AF505930

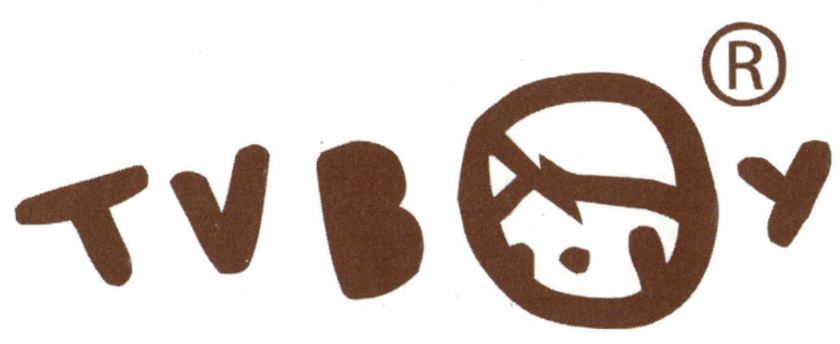

Start a Revolution without Weapons

DRAGO

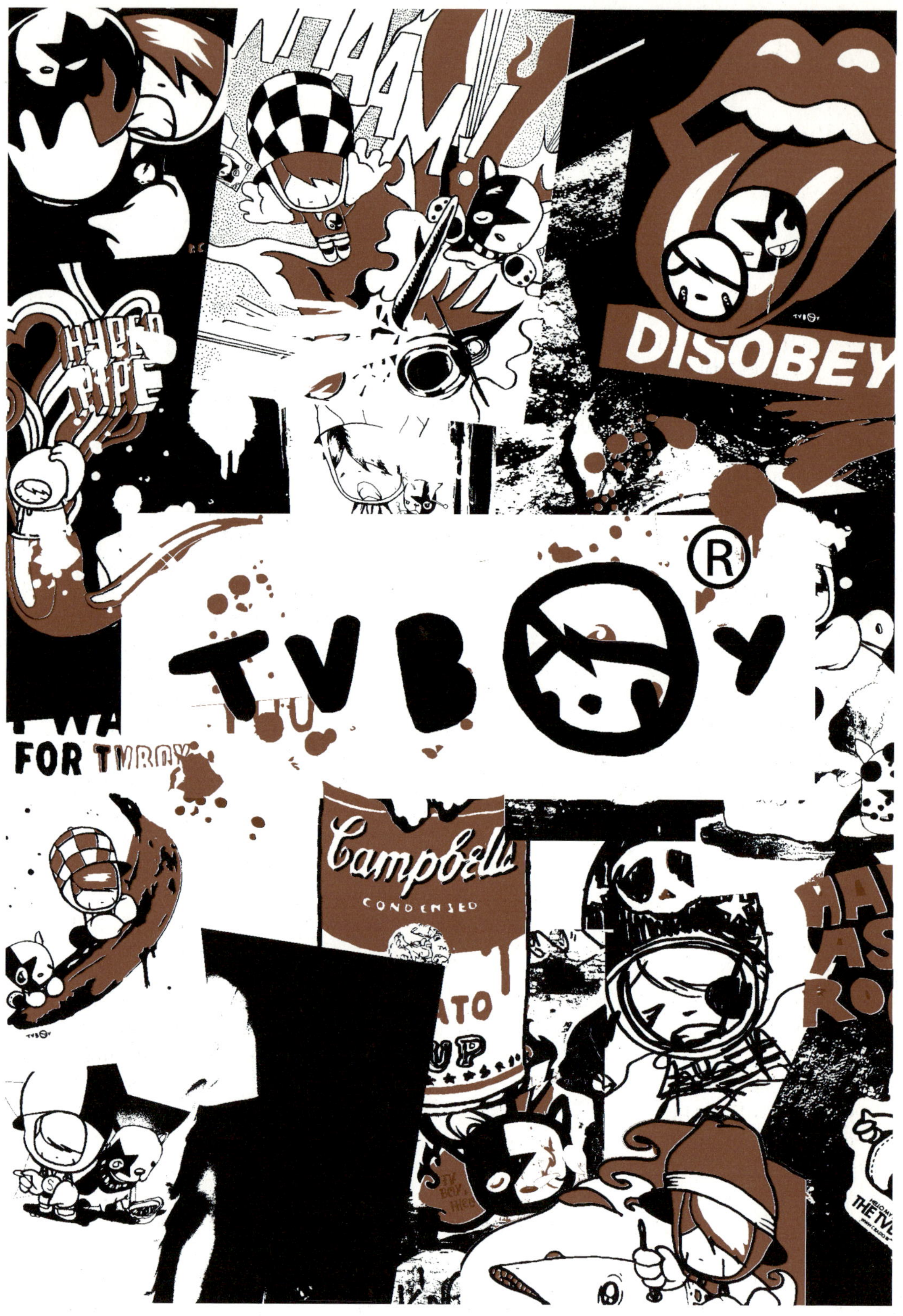

WHAAM!
HYPER PIPE
DISOBEY
FOR TVBOY
TVBOY
®
Campbell's
CONDENSED
TOMATO SOUP

Mash Up Boy

di Jacopo Perfetti

TvBoy is the son of post-modernism and of the cross-media mash-up. His works are a Bakhtinian carnivalization of the contemporary world, where styles, citations and influences pour onto his canvases like fragments of street pop with a neo-punk aftertaste. Starting with the streets as his own channel of expression, Salvatore Benintende, alias TvBoy, has made his art an ongoing experimentation with the idioms of communication, with mass media serving at the same time as the inspiration and the negation of his research. "Switch off the tv, you're the one on stage". With this message, simple and universally understandable, the artist has given life to his creative alter ego, a child observing with genuine sensitivity a present broken into an impure flux of mixed-up styles. All of these elements can be found in Salvatore's, whether they are on the street or in the studio. Looking at his canvases is like watching Peter Greenaway's "A Zed and Two Noughts" or Quentin Tarantino's "Pulp Fiction" through the fragmented filter of cyber-navigation. His art is a meta-narration of the contemporary, composed of reminders from a past revived in a game for two, where the spectator is invited to take part in the dialogue of Art. TvBoy has reinterpreted all his heroes, from Roy Lichtenstein to Milton Glaser, from Salvador Dalì to Andy Warhol, in a constant customization of his own history. In his canvases, the spirit of rock – the grunge of Guns and Roses and Nirvana – moves through the fetishes of pop iconography in an ironical *assemblage* in the style of Adrian Tranquilli. As the postmodern artist mixes anthropological symbols and religious archetypes into comic book superheroes and iconography, TvBoy uses the same irony in reflecting on figures characterizing his era, alluding to an uncertainty typical of this century, where "everything is possible and nothing is true". The essence of his art lies precisely in the sensibility with which he observes the reality surrounding him. This genuine and almost adolescent sensibility, leads him to be astonished by the Other who becomes, in his canvases, the dialectical instrument of his art. From the irony of postmodernism and to the capacity of mixing styles and instruments typical of the media mash up, the artist adds all the expressive energy of street art, a movement he adopted at the very beginning. On the street, Salvatore wears the clothes of TvBoy, a personality lost midway between the tenderness of the child and the explosiveness of the *illustrarocker*, who leaves his mark traveling from the streets of Milan, where it is easy to see his works, often flanked by those of other street artists, to the periphery of Barcelona, which the artist has chosen as his creative *atelier*. Thus his art becomes public art, which everyone can enjoy, and it surprises and provokes, narrates and astonishes. Thanks to his uniqueness, he manages to stand up against the *anti-graffito* terrorism dominating Milan in this period, when, without making any distinctions, the wall surfaces of the city were being restored to the same colour gray as the city atmosphere. The best way to get acquainted with the art of TvBoy is to walk through the streets of the cities which have welcomed him, cities which the artist has donated corners of color, from the graffito created with the street poet Ivan in Via Cassala, in Milan, to the landslide of stickers TvBoy has used to customize cities all over Europe. Salvatore generates his art both in galleries and on the street, imagining dream worlds and engendering visions as he slides, with exquisite balance, between art and design, illustration and communication, inviting all to take part in his *revolution without weapons*. *Come out and play!*

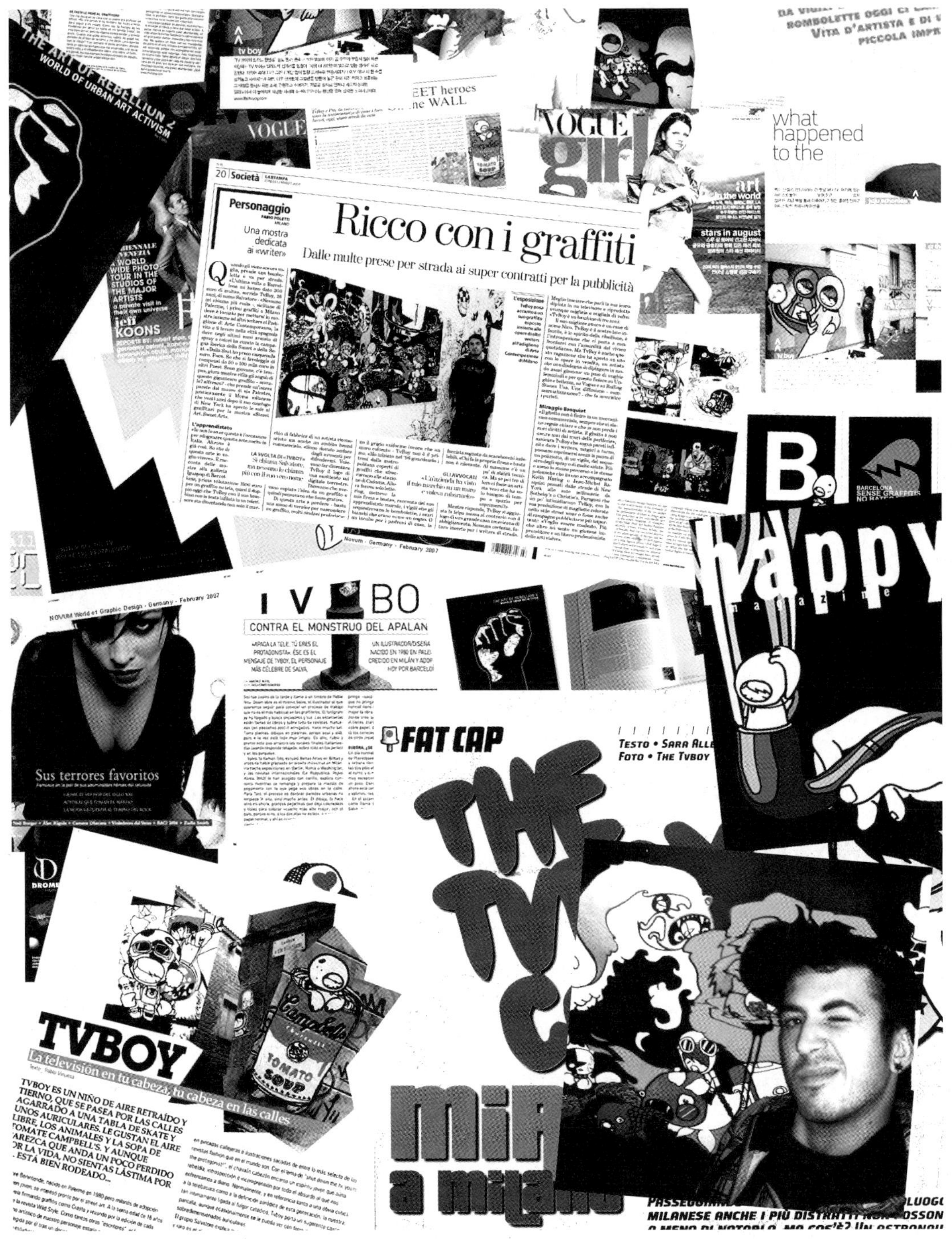

Press selection & Portrait of Tvboy in his studio - Barcelona 2007

Tributes

TV Boy is a large geezer. You rarely meet someone with the passion and enthusiasm he has and it was a pleasure to see his work all over Barcelona and Milan in recent years. I, for one, am looking forward to a copy of the book. I hope one day to pass it on to my children who I hope will pass it on to their children but who will probably sell it because they'll need the money because it will be worth thousands of euros in the future if there is not an impending nuclear war.
Chaz / *The London Police (NL)*

I hate the announcer of Wheel of Fortune and his silicon bitch. I can't stand the smiling guy from the news who looks like Barbie's boyfriend. I don't want to watch more Junk-food TV commercials during my son's cartoons. But that TV Boy is different from them, he doesn't try to tell me the new president is good for me. Or that I should buy that new computer that I don't really need. He is just there like a good old friend.
Eko / *ekosystem.org (FRA)*

TV Boy swings between art and design and is well aware of the downside of both, the unpredictability of the art market and the enslavement of talent in design agencies. His preference is for a reproducible art in the simple language of *"fumetto"*. His fresh ideas for images have already landed him prestigious commissions. But what brought him to the Iberian peninsula from Italy? What else but *amor*. A superb basis for further flights of fantasy.
Susanne Schaller / *Novum Magazine (DE)*

His art between boundaries is eye-catching and suggestive, appealing already in its most simple form. TV Boy is currently in a very interesting moment in his career, jumping from the design and street to the gallery scene. In this impasse important things have already begun to happen in his work, like the development in the use of colour, a bigger depth -both pictorial and conceptual-, and the warm feeling that he is increasingly leaving space for his sensitiveness to invade his art. I'm very excited to see what will come in the next few years.
Inigo Martinez Moller / *Iguapop Gallery (ESP)*

For better (maybe) and worse (clearly) TV has changed since Poltergeist and we're all lost in and behind screens, unable to measure the impact, influence, or pure illusion generated from this ubiquitous blue light. Unless of course, we switch it off, dazzle and destroy with a playful politic. I don't know TV Boy. Still, like that old boob tube I know the boy gets around and gives it his own slant. His characters have been there to welcome me to cities I did not know, to provide familiar faces; a silent presence laughing between all the commercials and putting bubbles back into pop. No soda, no chips, no potatoes, you can keep walking, you can jump and pull or simply pass by, but what he offered takes more energy, more risk and more love than zoning out to the sound of zap zap zap. Is it art? Is it design? Is it advertising? I don't care. "Just Do It" made sense before Nike transformed it.
Harlan Levey / *Director of Modart Magazine (BE)*

CNN, MTV, VH1, ...there are many TV stations but there is only one TV Boy. This guy knows how to take over the streets. Though I only met TV Boy a few times in person I recognised his spray painted TV Boy in cities such as Milan and Barcelona many many times. You should watch out for this guy!
Christian Hundertmark / *Author of the "The Art of Rebellion" (DE)*

His big headed children with the face fitted in a TV screen have a Kauai grace that reminds me of Aya Katano and the others Japanese artists from Kiki Kaikai, Takashi Murakami's Factory. But Salvatore, born in Palermo, raised in Milan and now based in Barcelona, found his influences in the occidental tradition of comic strips, with authors such as Schultz and Watterson.
Fabia di Drusco / *Vogue Uomo (ITA)*

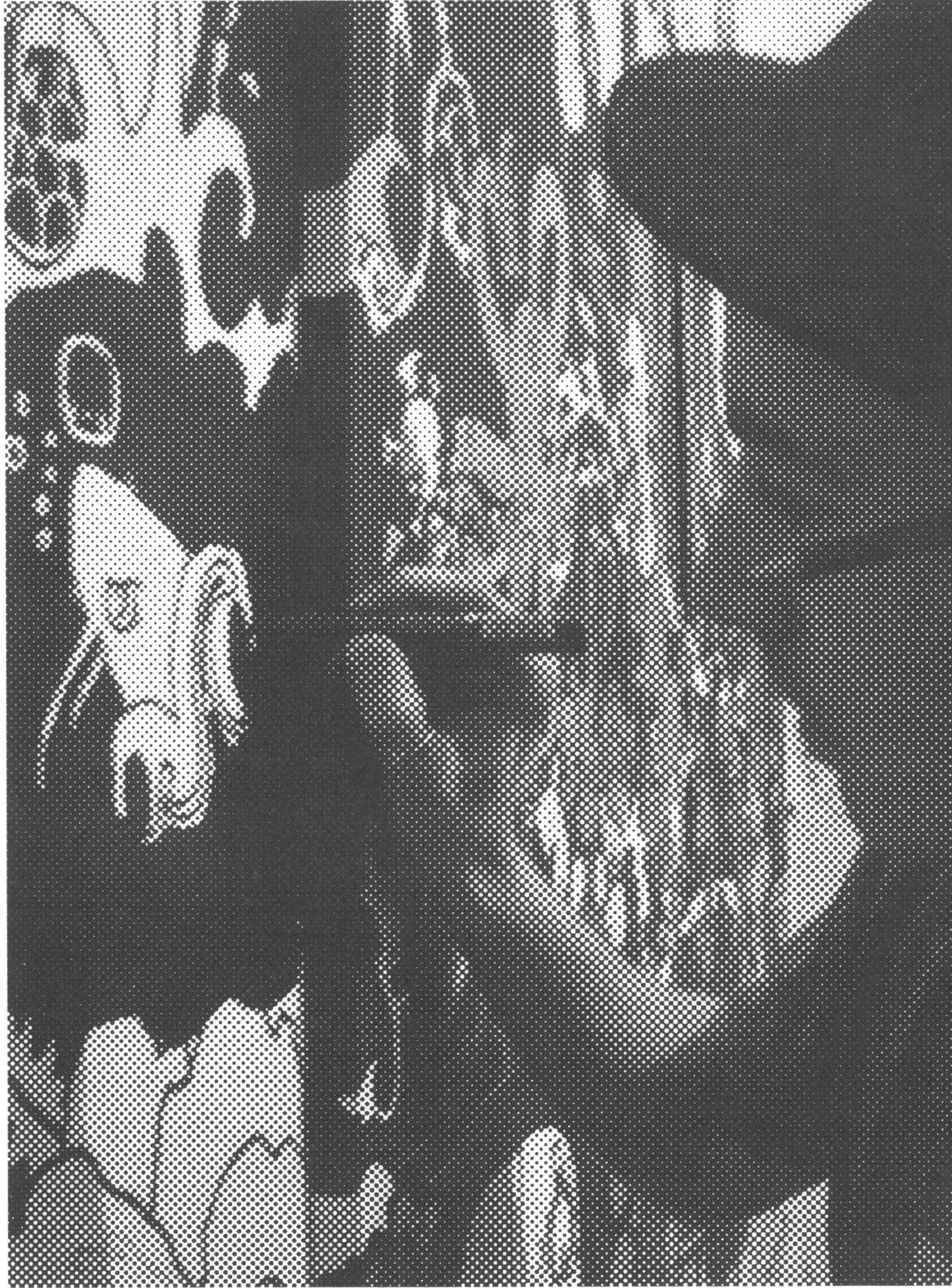

FINE ART

Start a Revolution without Weapons

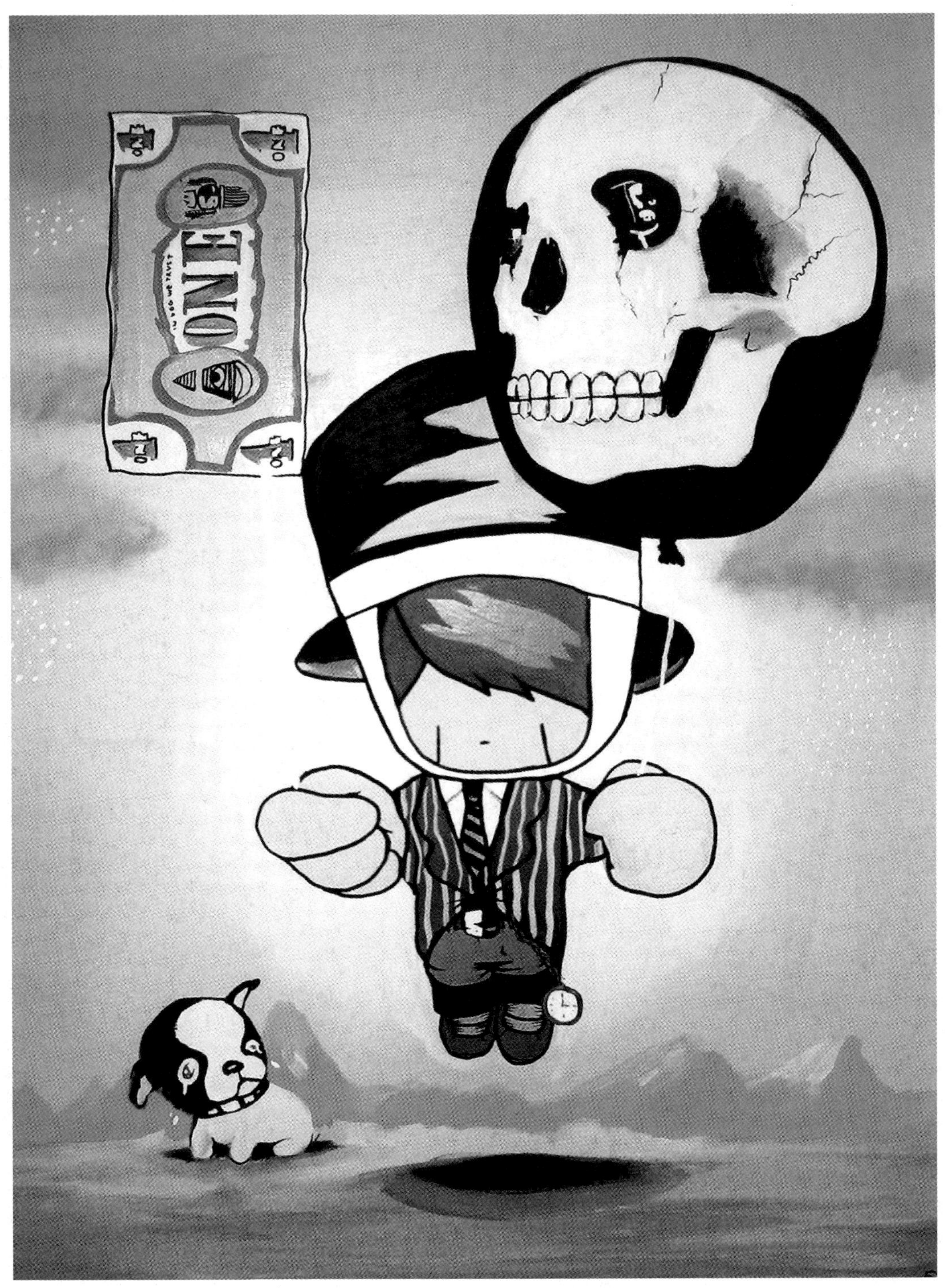

Please don't die - mixed media on canvas - 100x80 cm - 2007

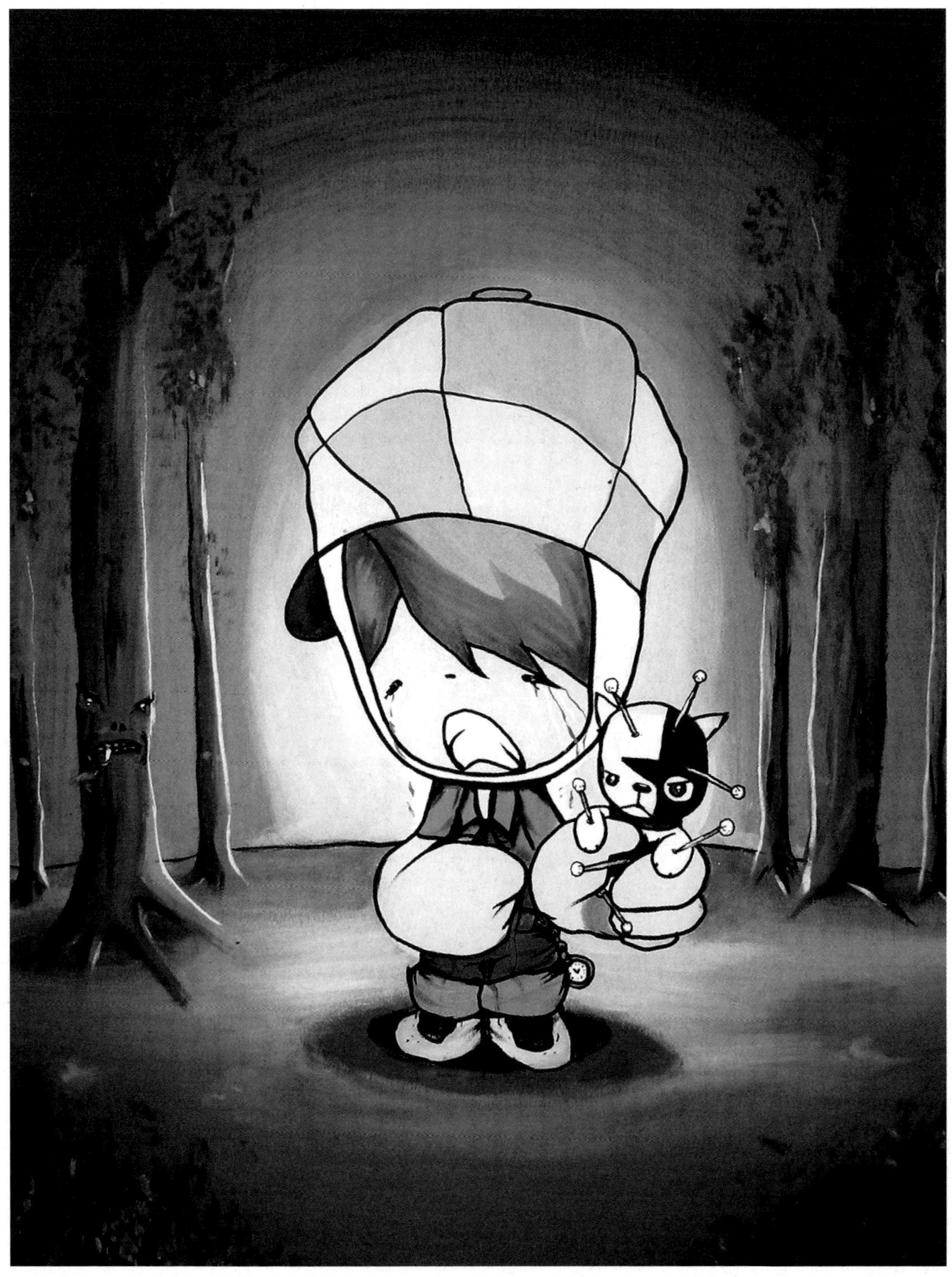

Voodoo - mixed media on canvas - 100x80 cm - 2007

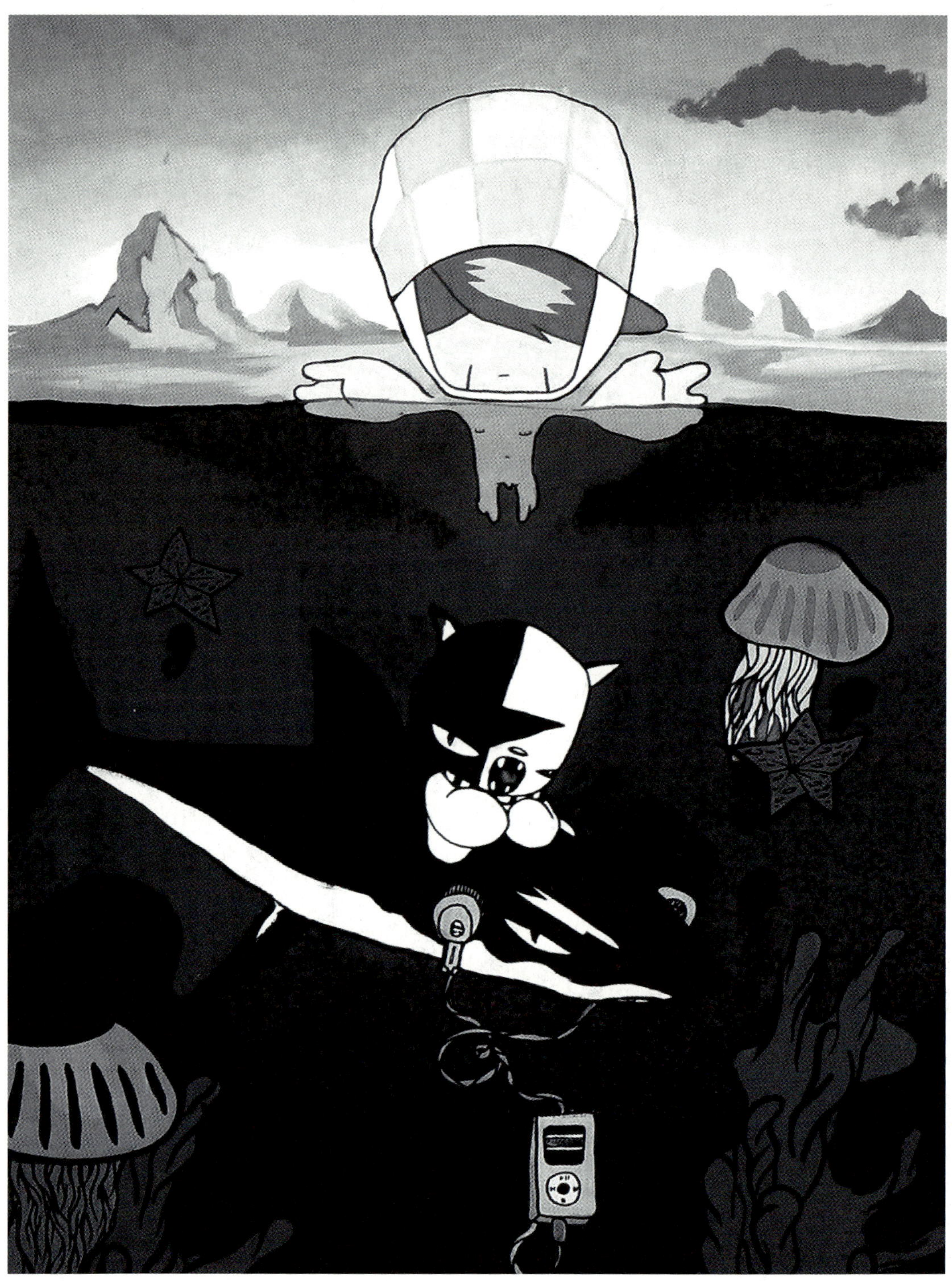

Killing me softly - mixed media on canvas - 146x114 cm - 2007

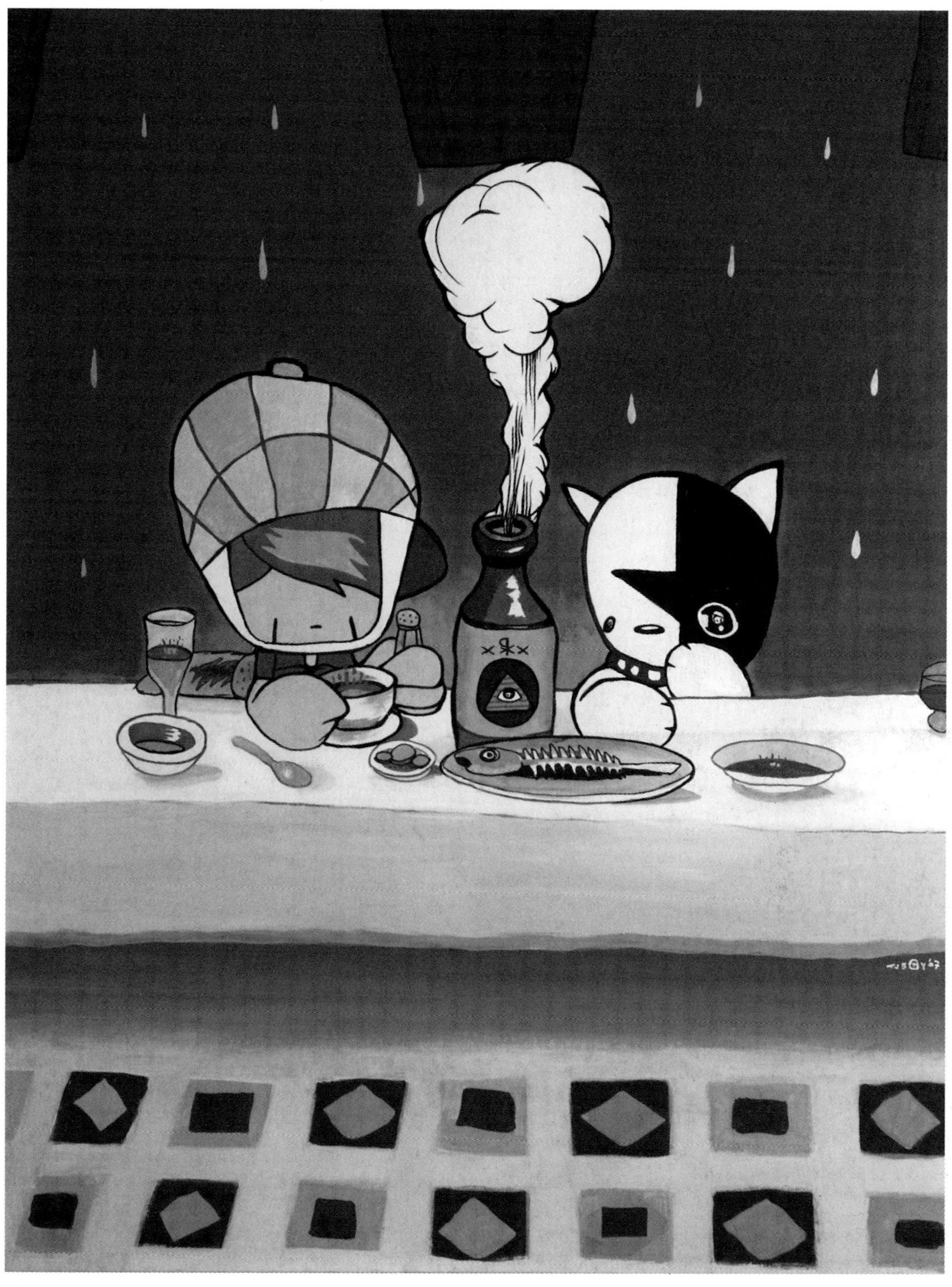

The Last Supper - mixed media on canvas - 146x114 cm - 2007

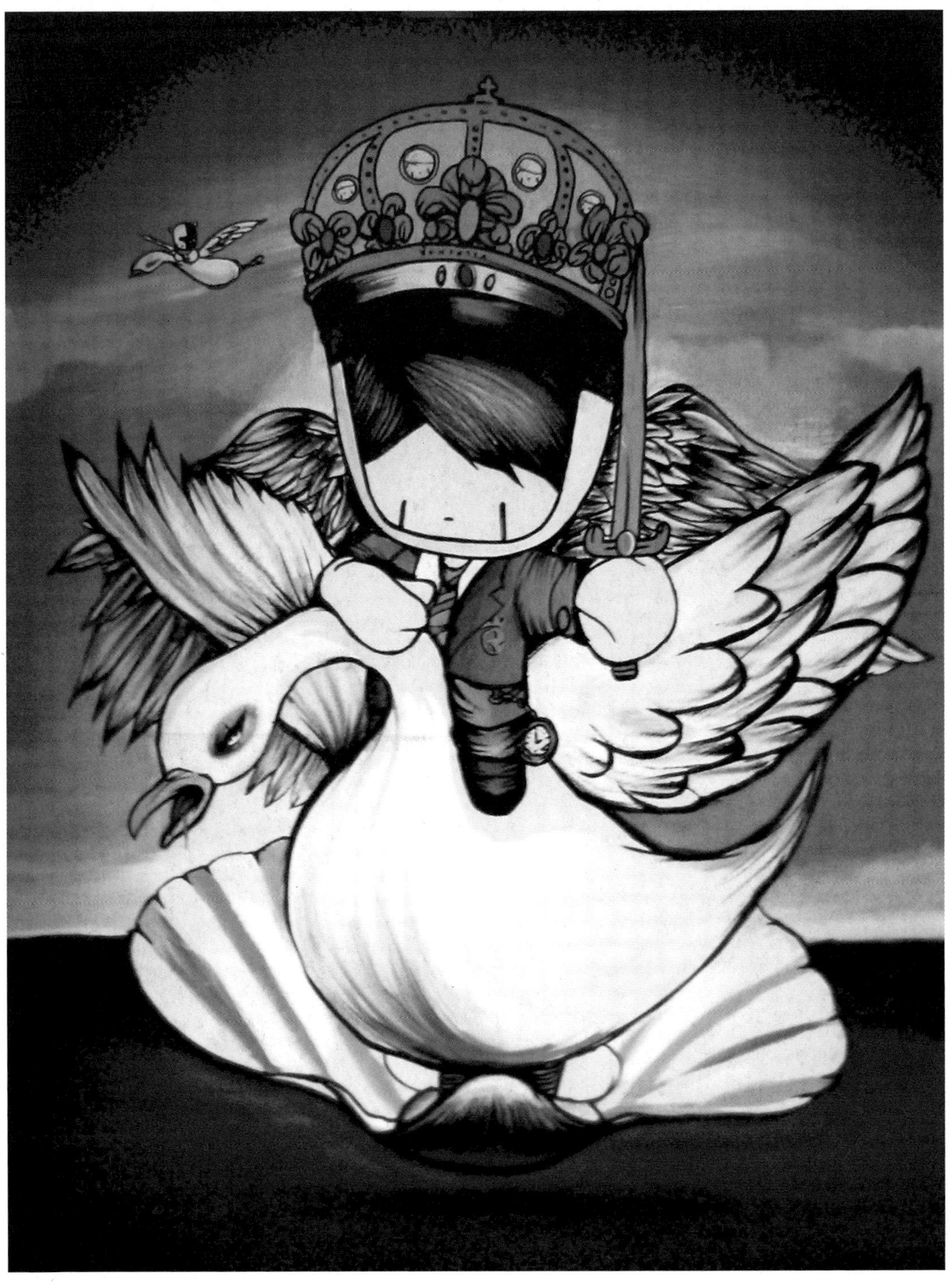

Rebirth - mixed media on canvas - 100x80 cm - 2007

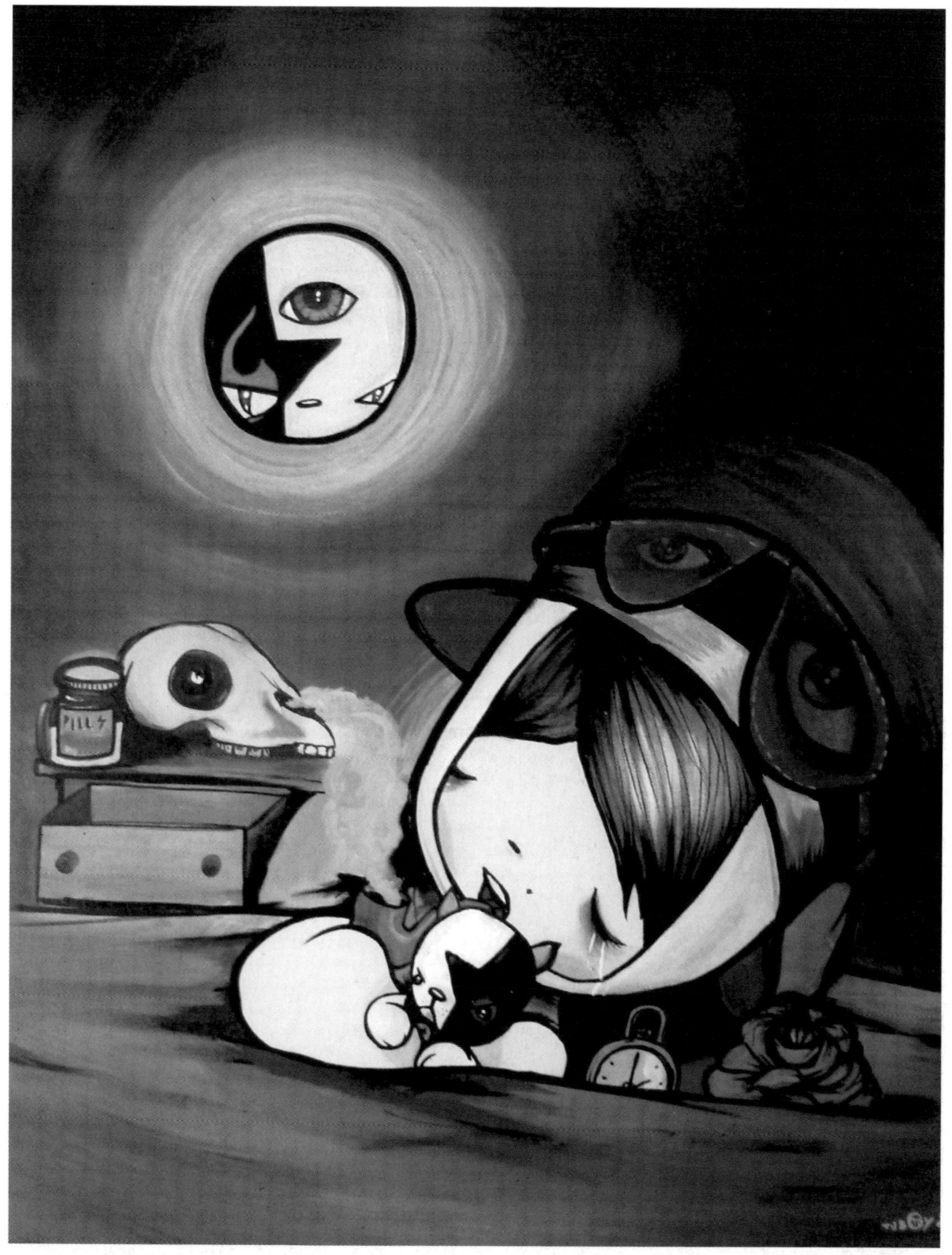

The Dream - mixed media on canvas - 100x80 cm - 2007

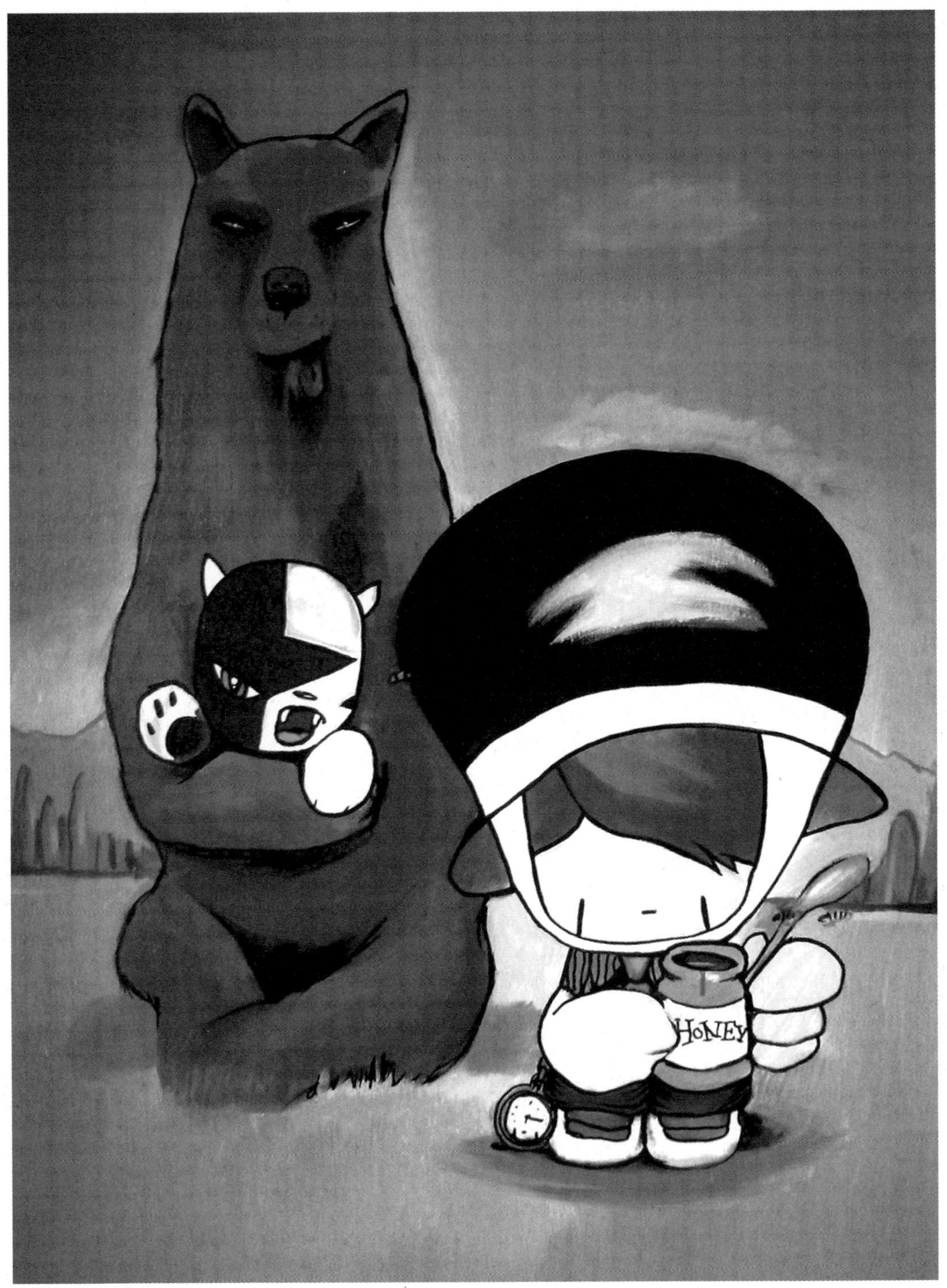

Honey   mixcd media on canvas - 100x80 cm - 200/

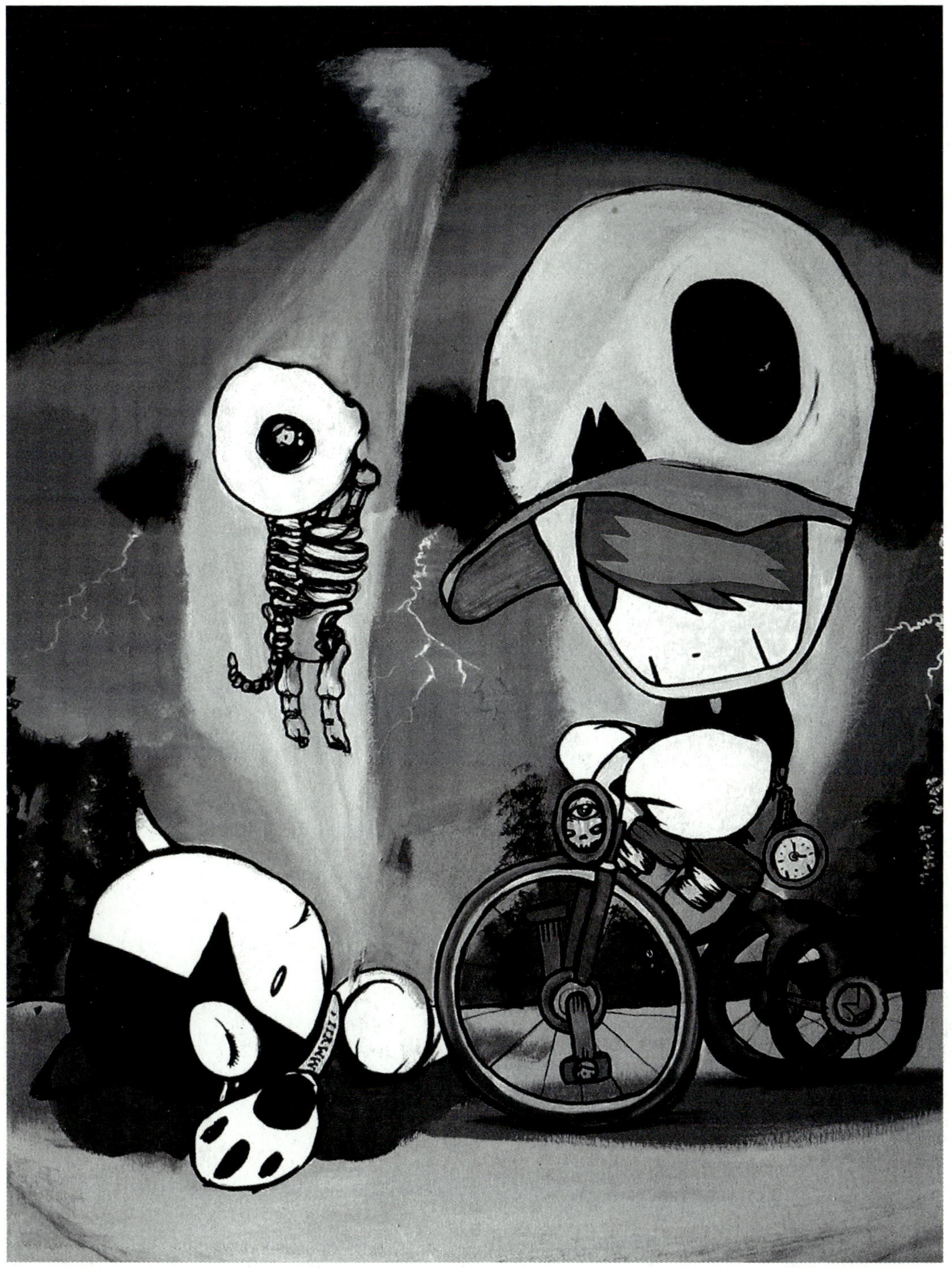

The Death of Nico - mixed media on canvas - 100x80 cm - 2007

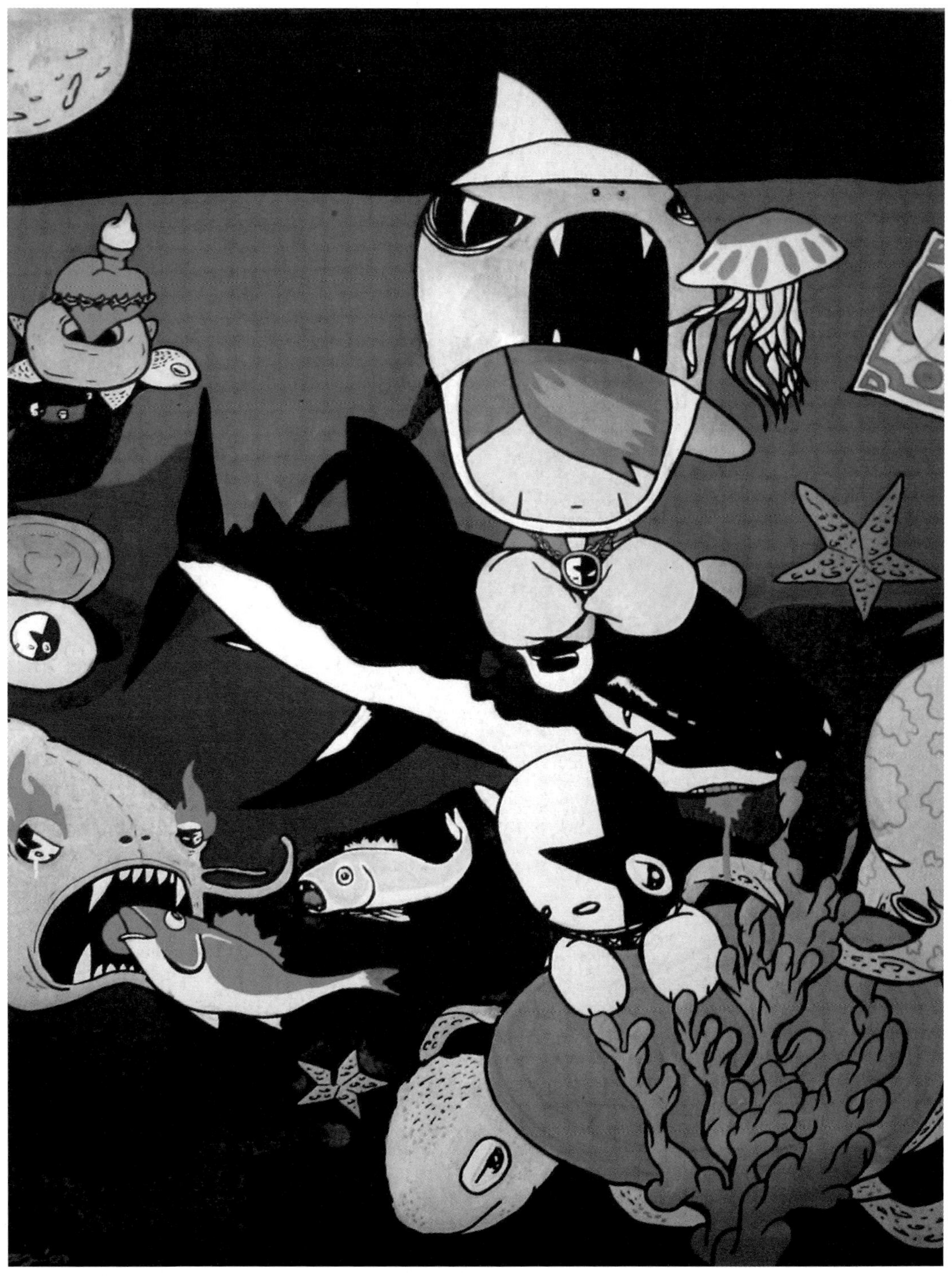

Under the Sea - mixed media on canvas - 100x80 cm - 2007

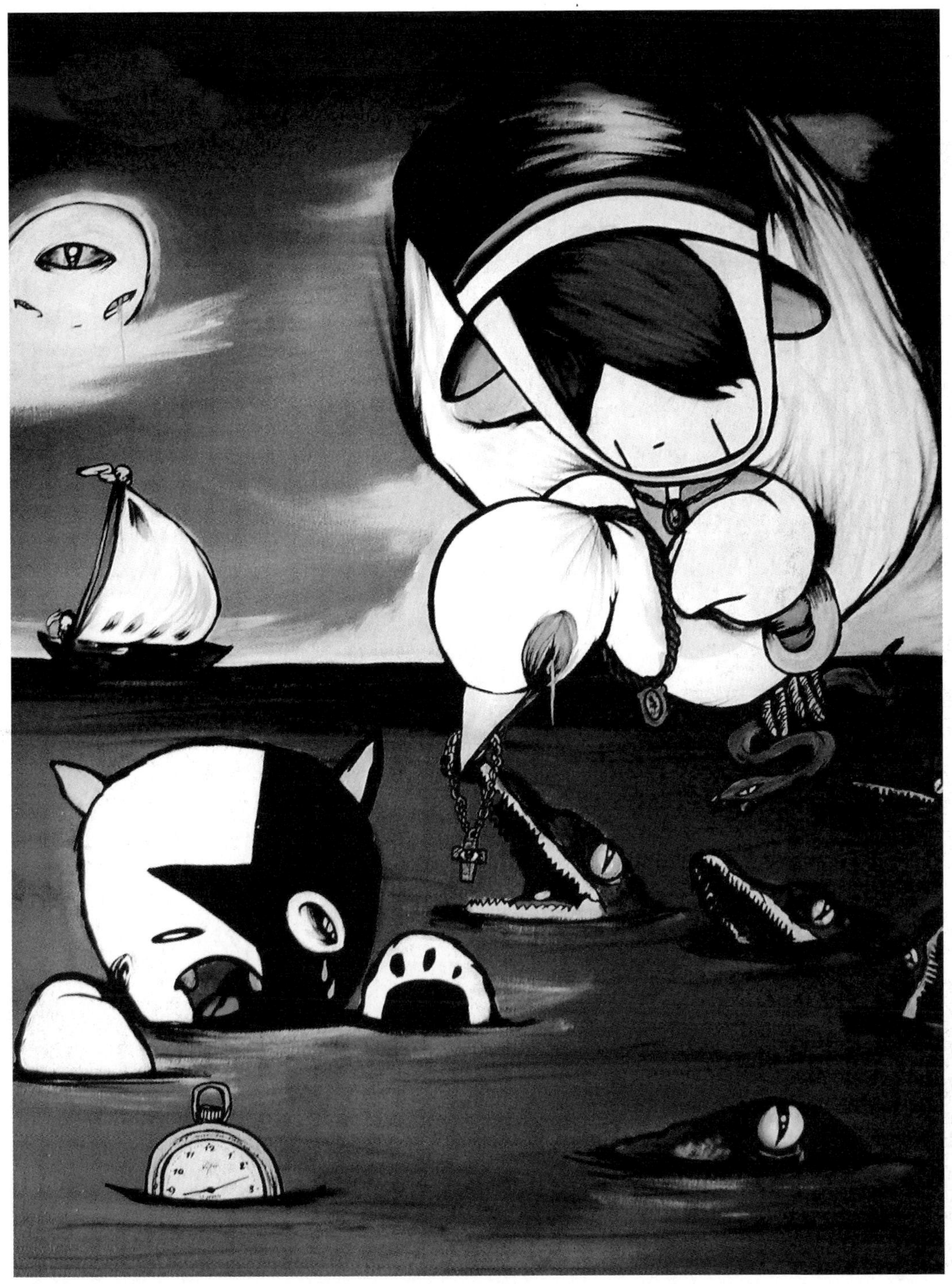

Time Hunters - mixed media on canvas - 100x80 cm - 2007

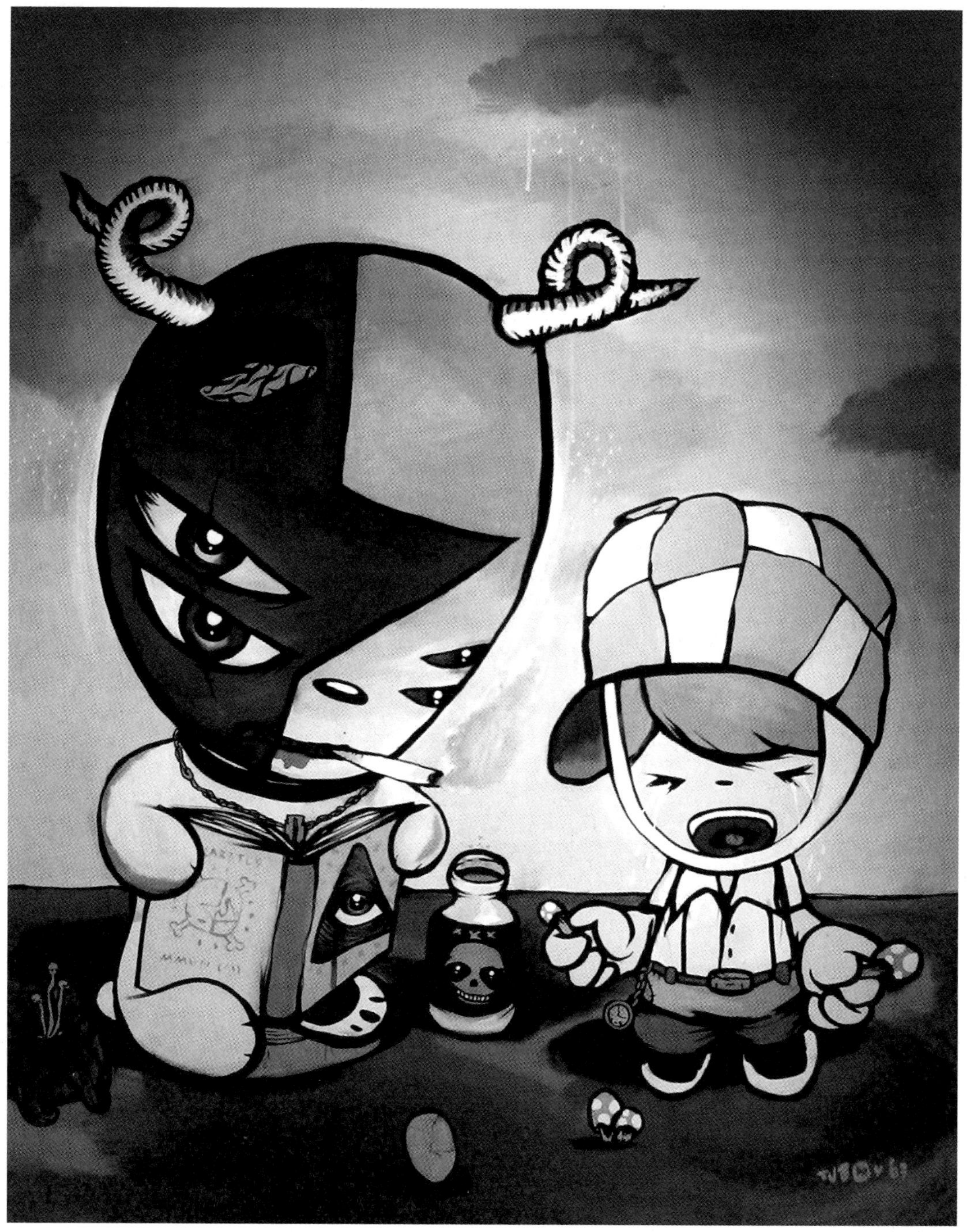

Scary Tales - mixed media on canvas - 146x114 cm - 2007

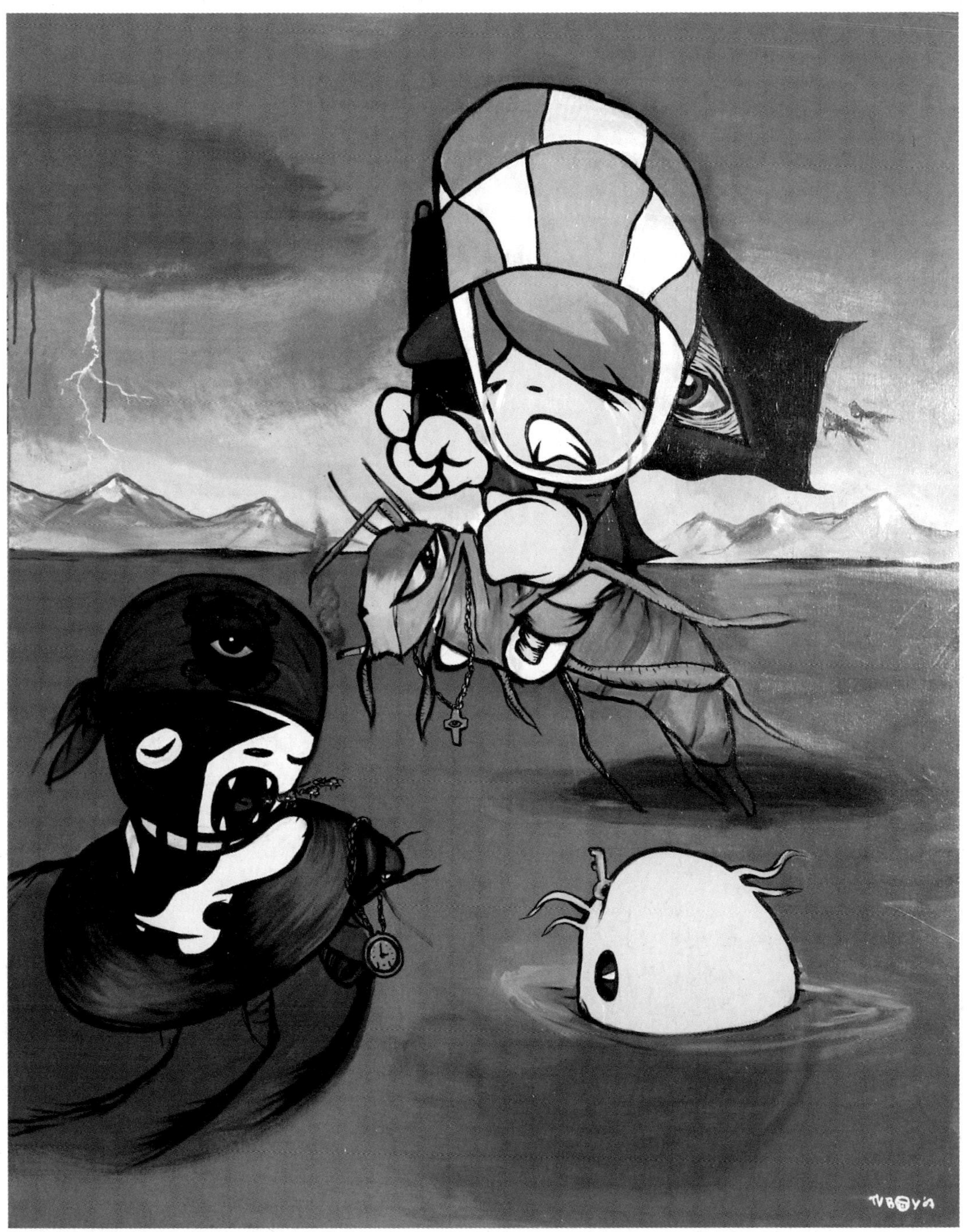

Cockroaches' Revenge - mixed media on canvas - 146x114 cm 2007

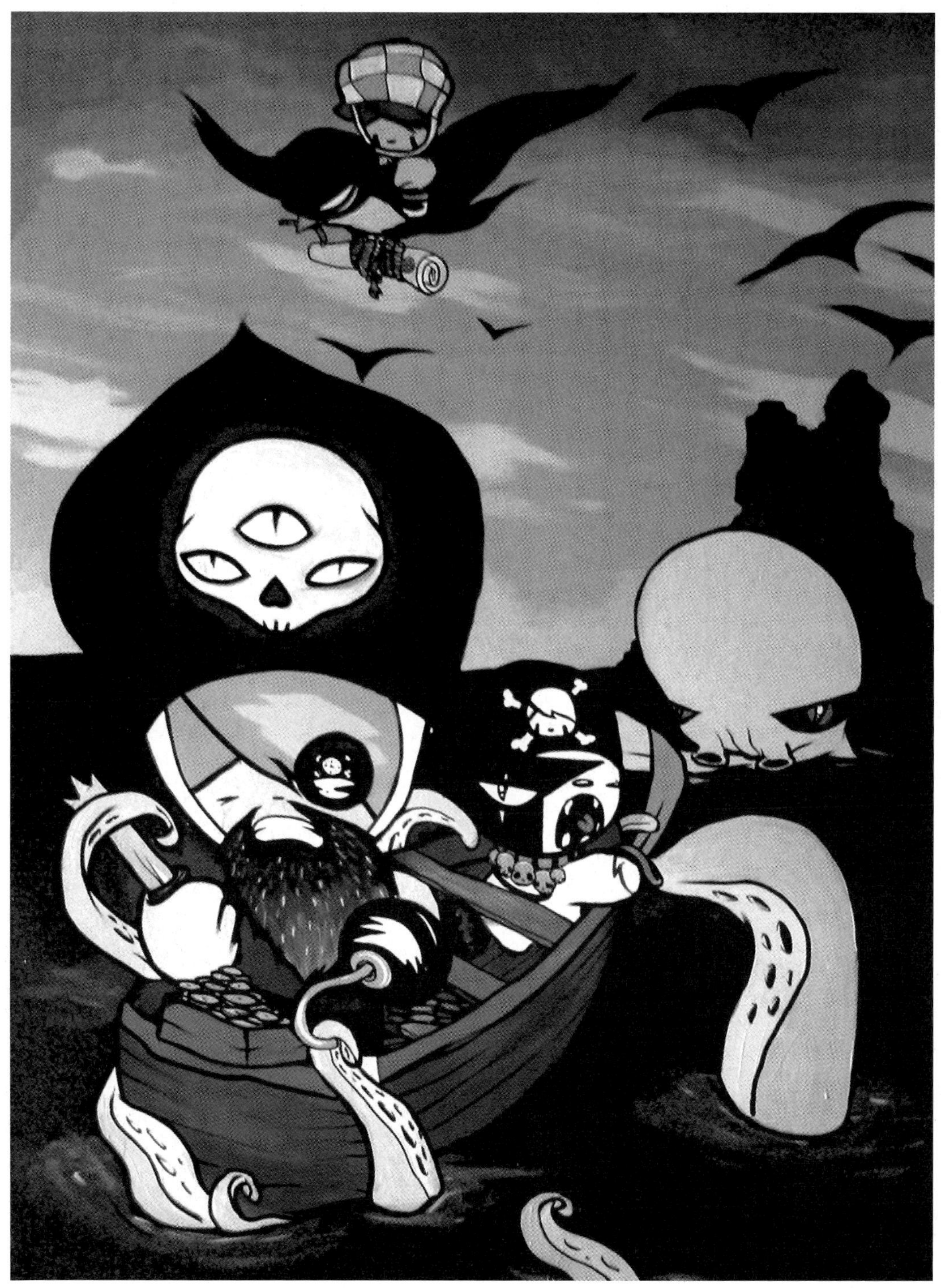

Haitian Shores - mixed media on canvas - 195x130 cm - 2007

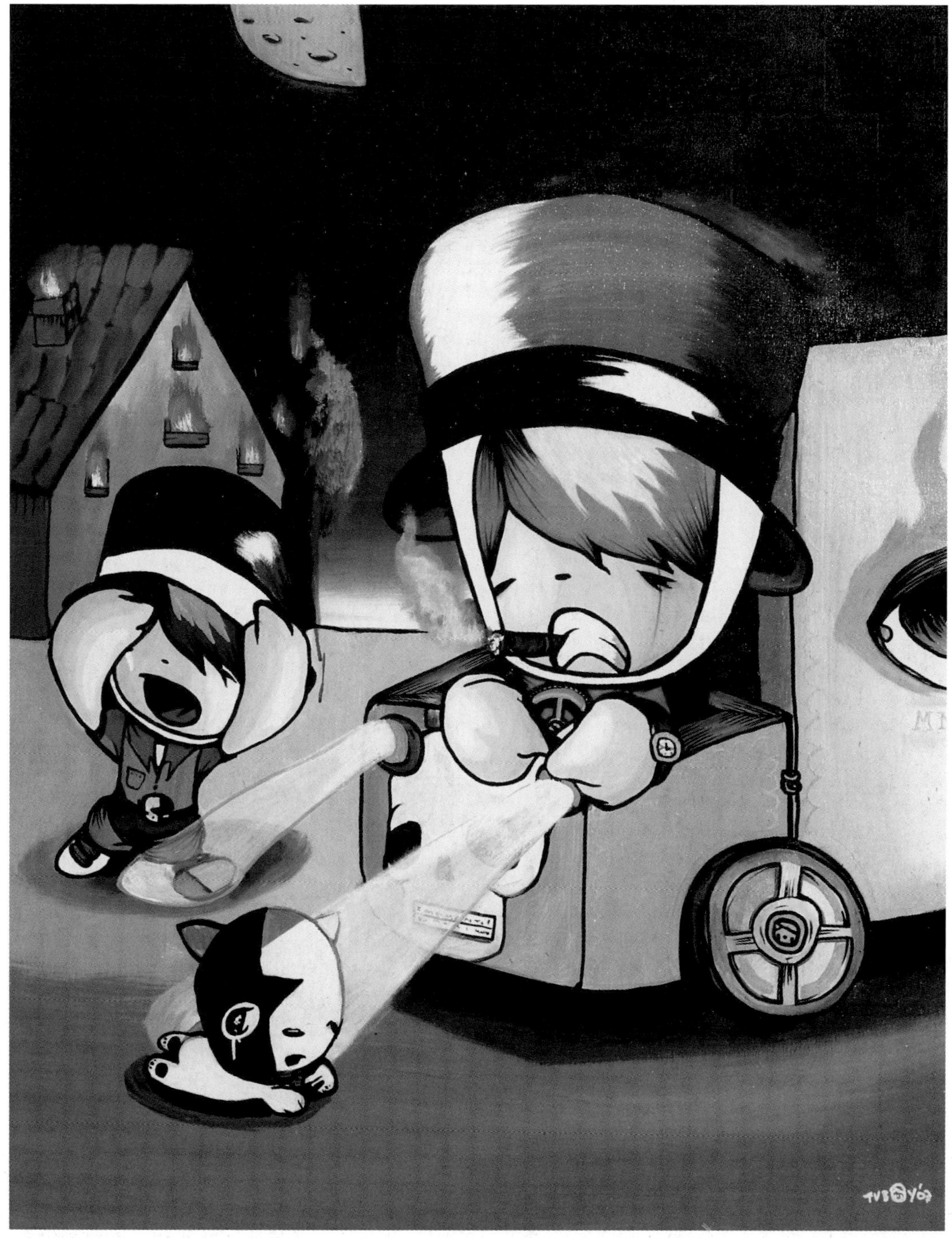

Memento Mori - mixed media on canvas - 100x80 cm - 2007

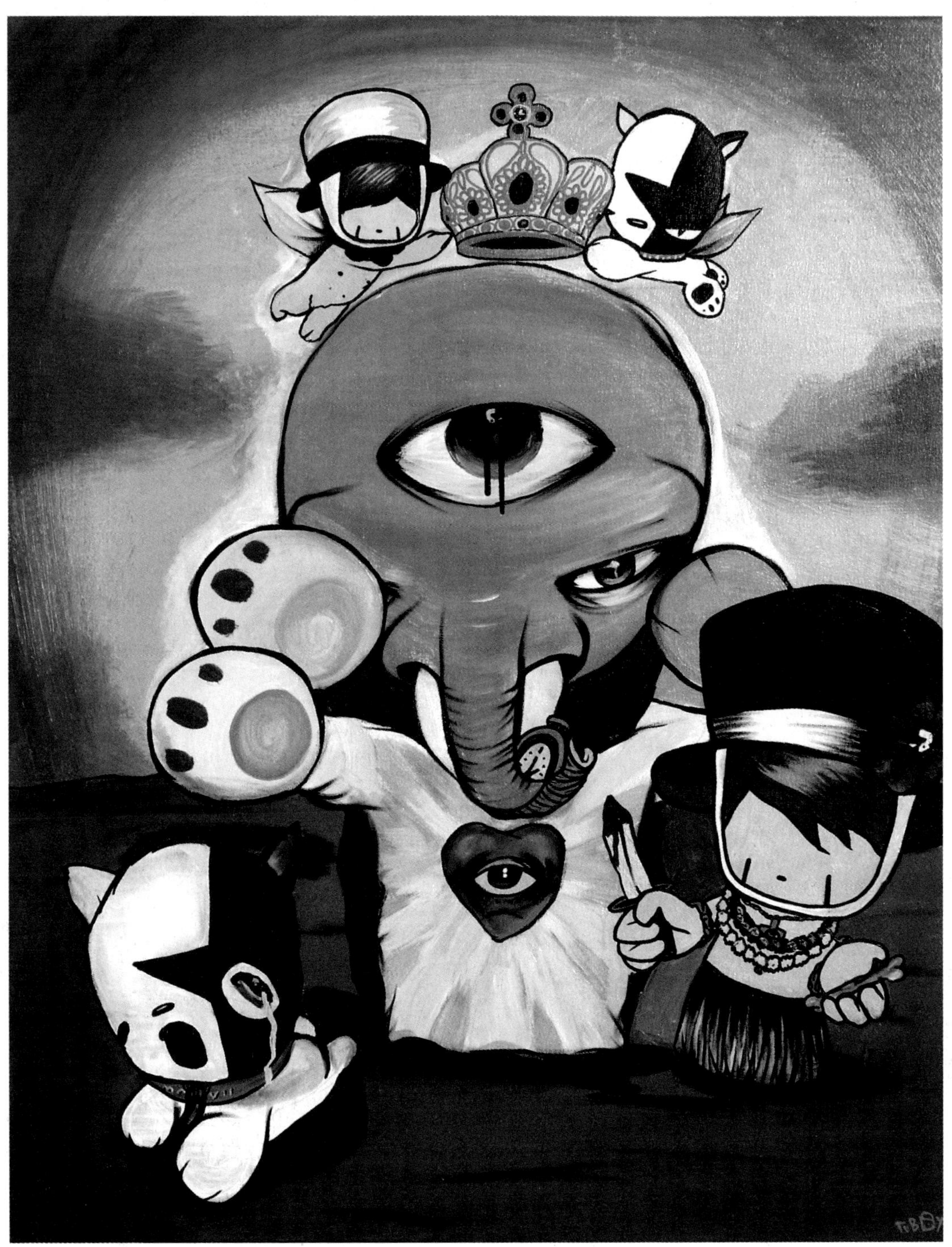

No Future - mixed media on canvas -100x80 cm - 2007

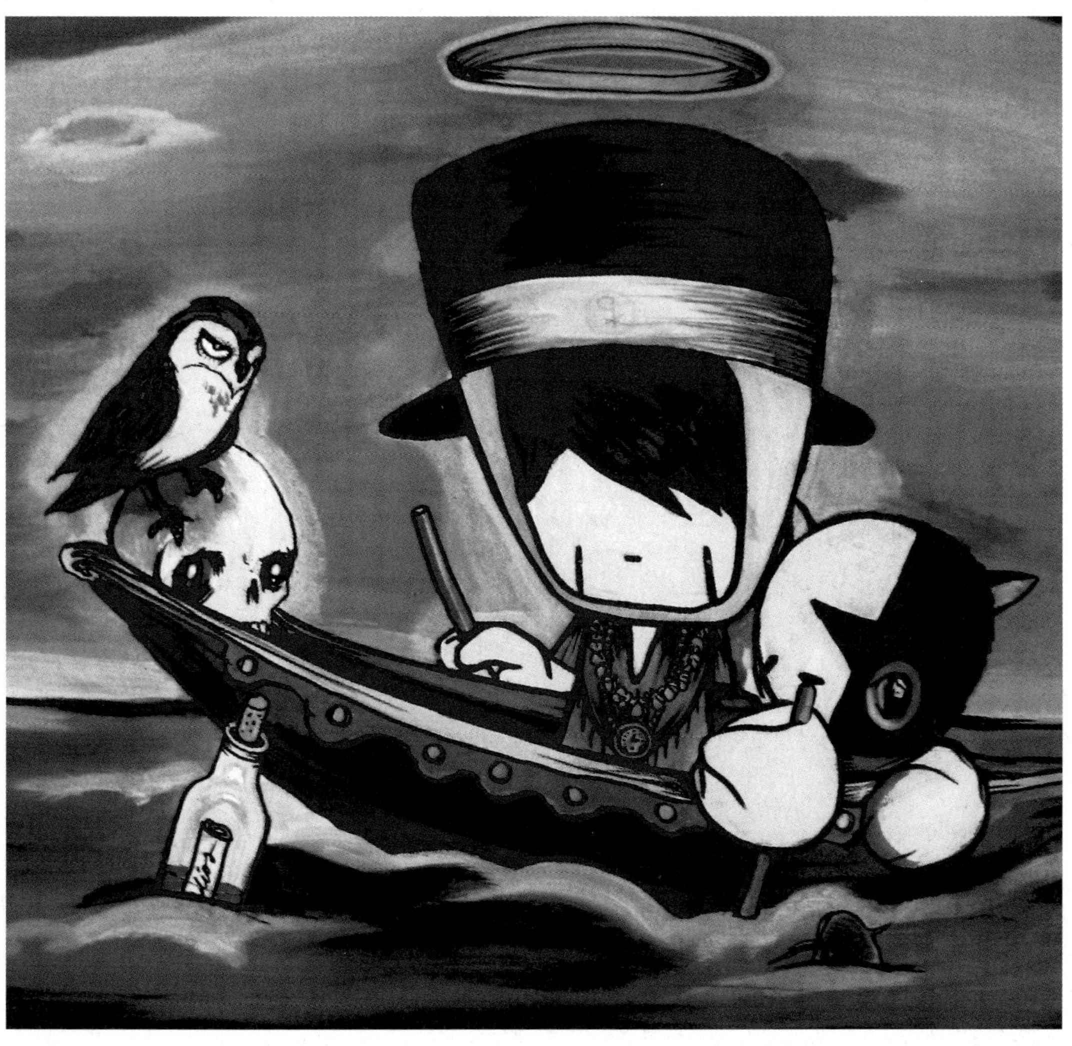

Adeusiau - mixed media on canvas - 63x70 cm - 2007

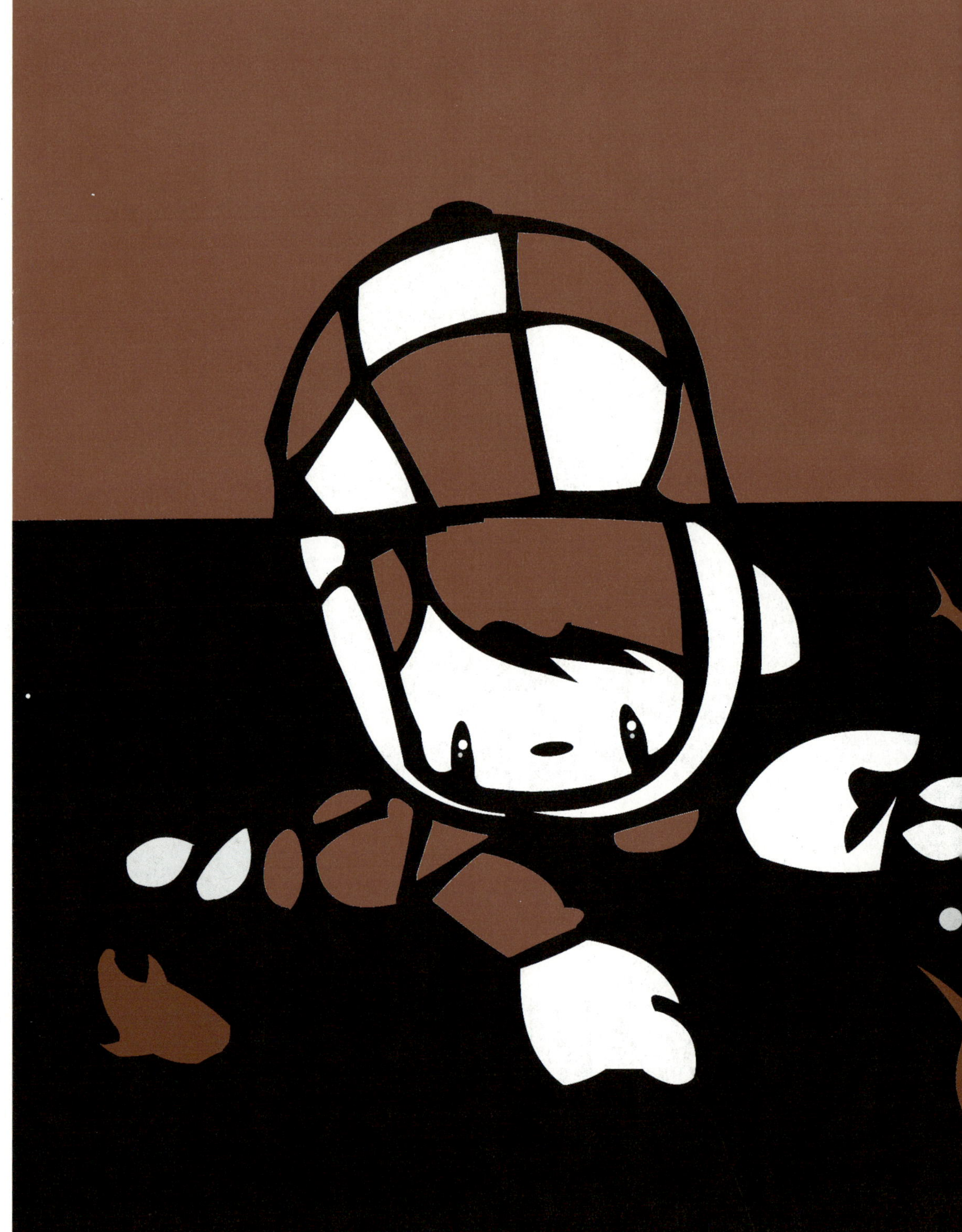

DRAWINGS

Start a Revolution without Weapons

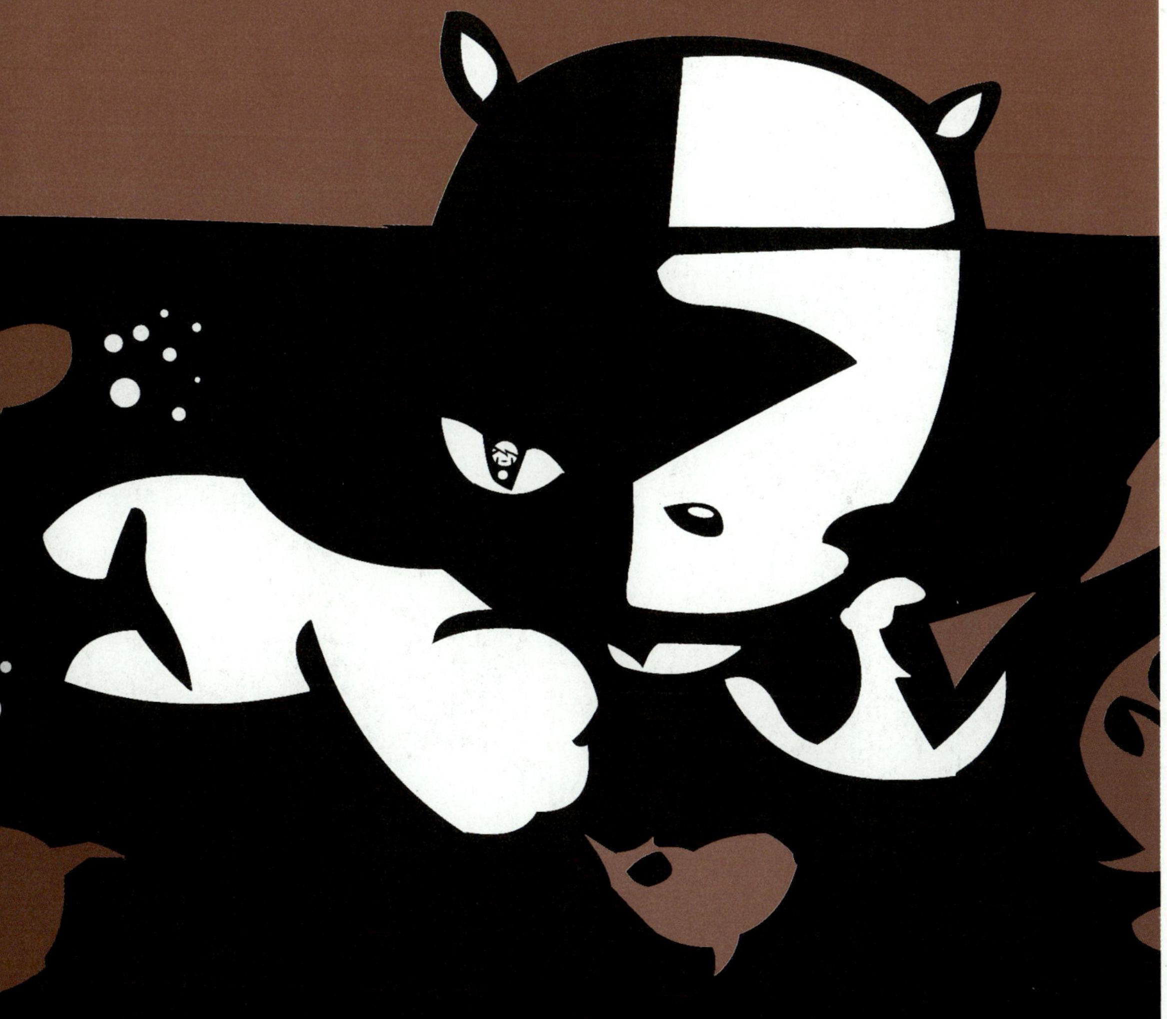

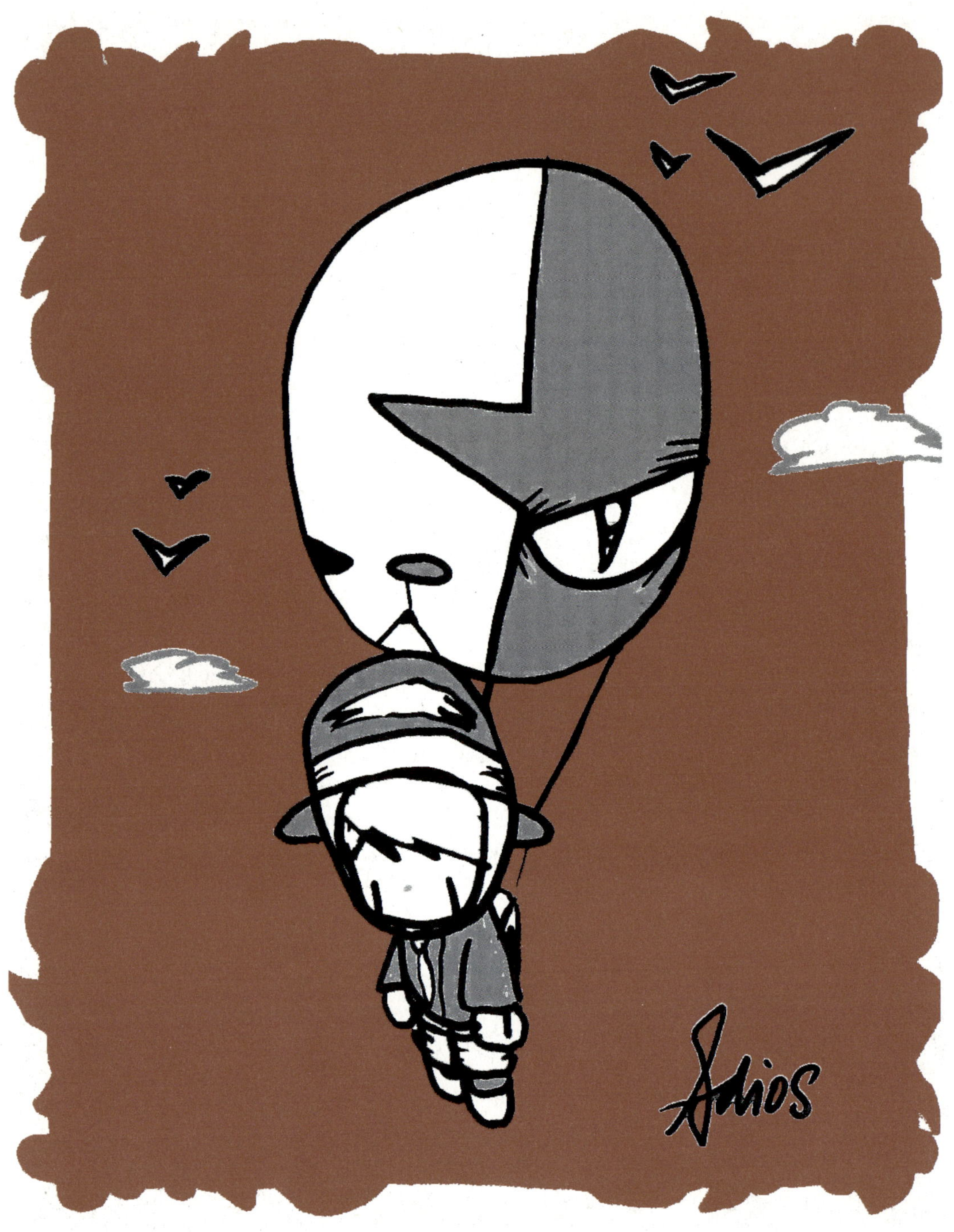

Adios - Ink on paper drawing - 40x30 cm - 2007

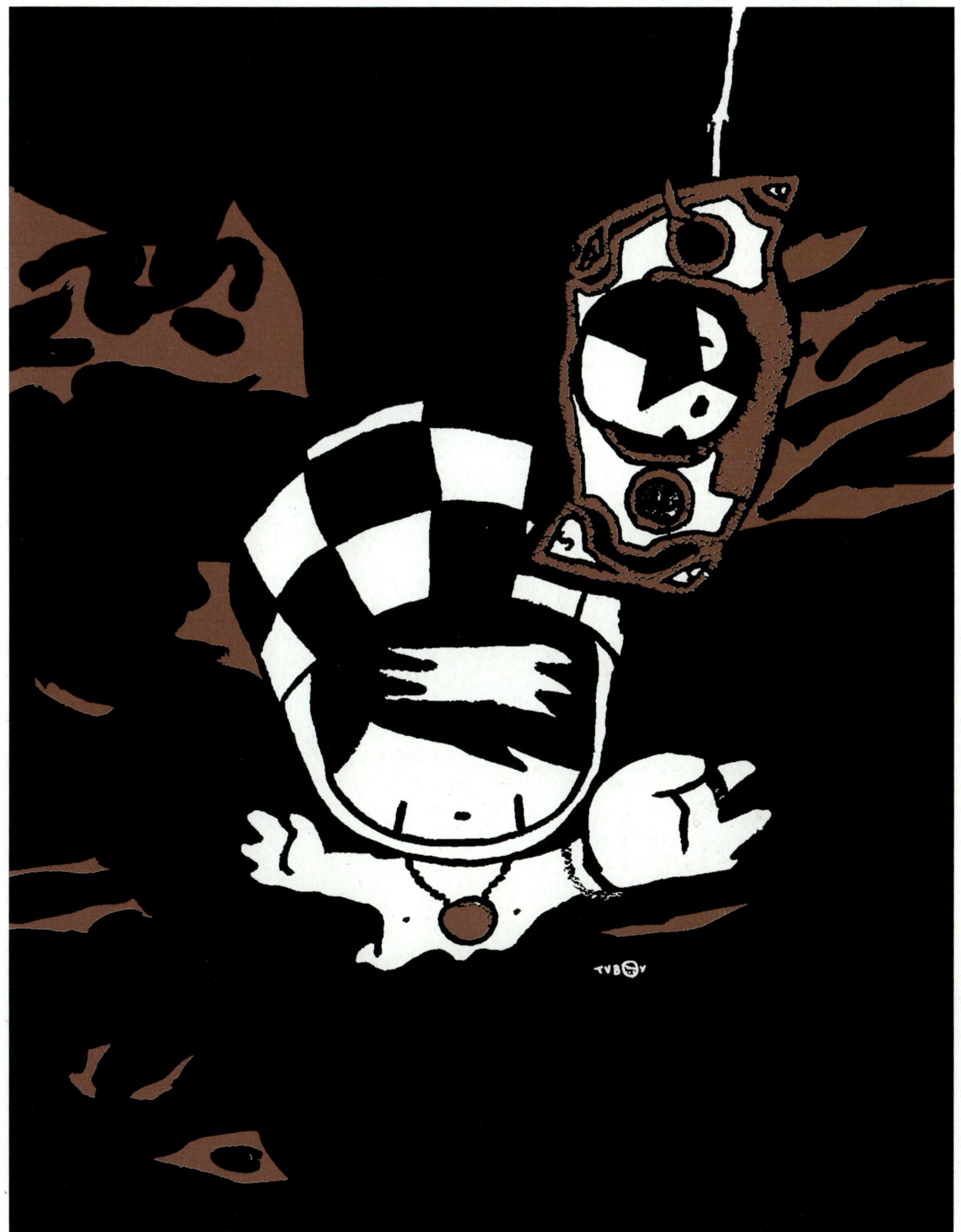

Nevermind - mixed media on canvas - 100x80 cm - 2007

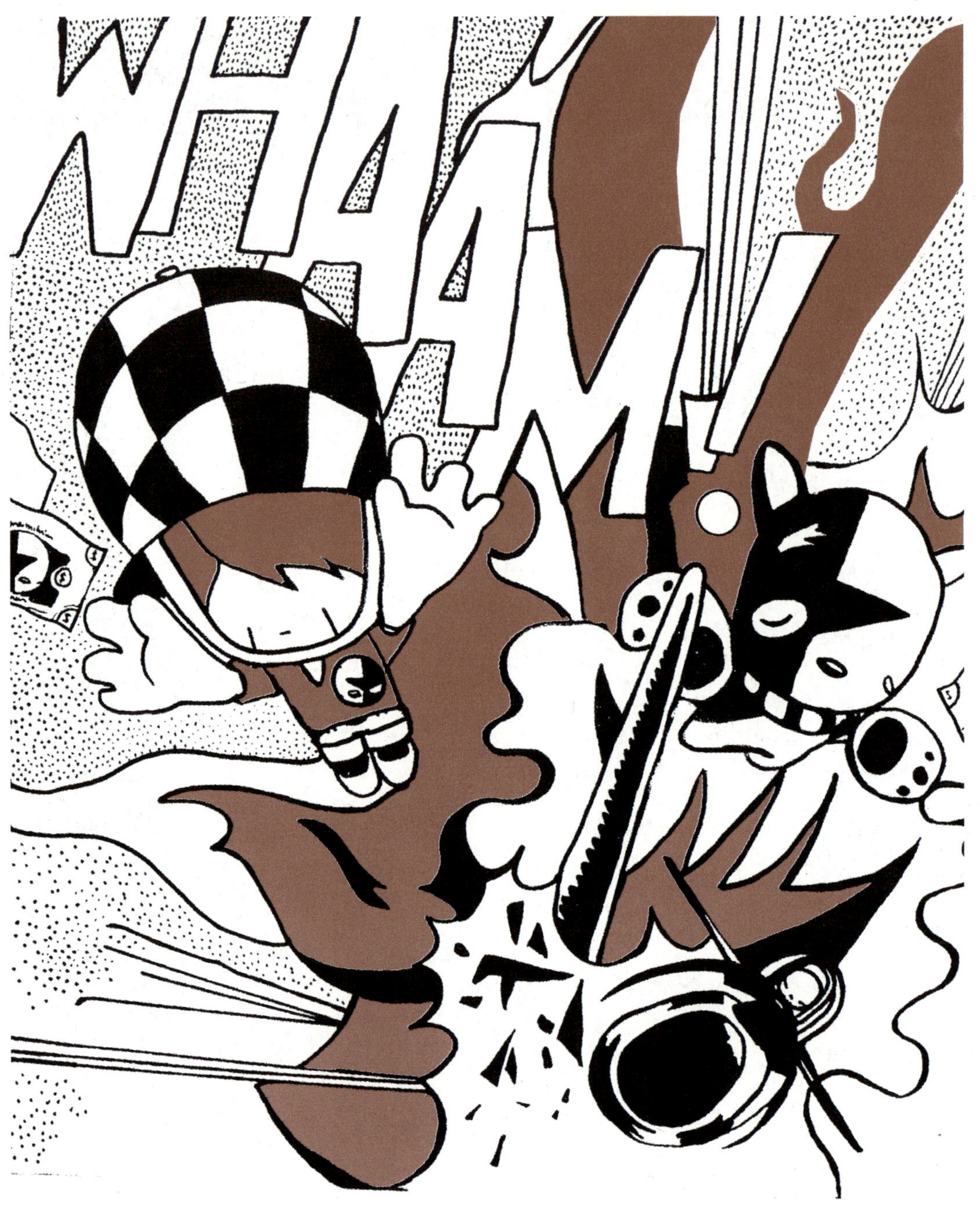

Whaam! - mixed media on canvas - 100x80 cm - 2007

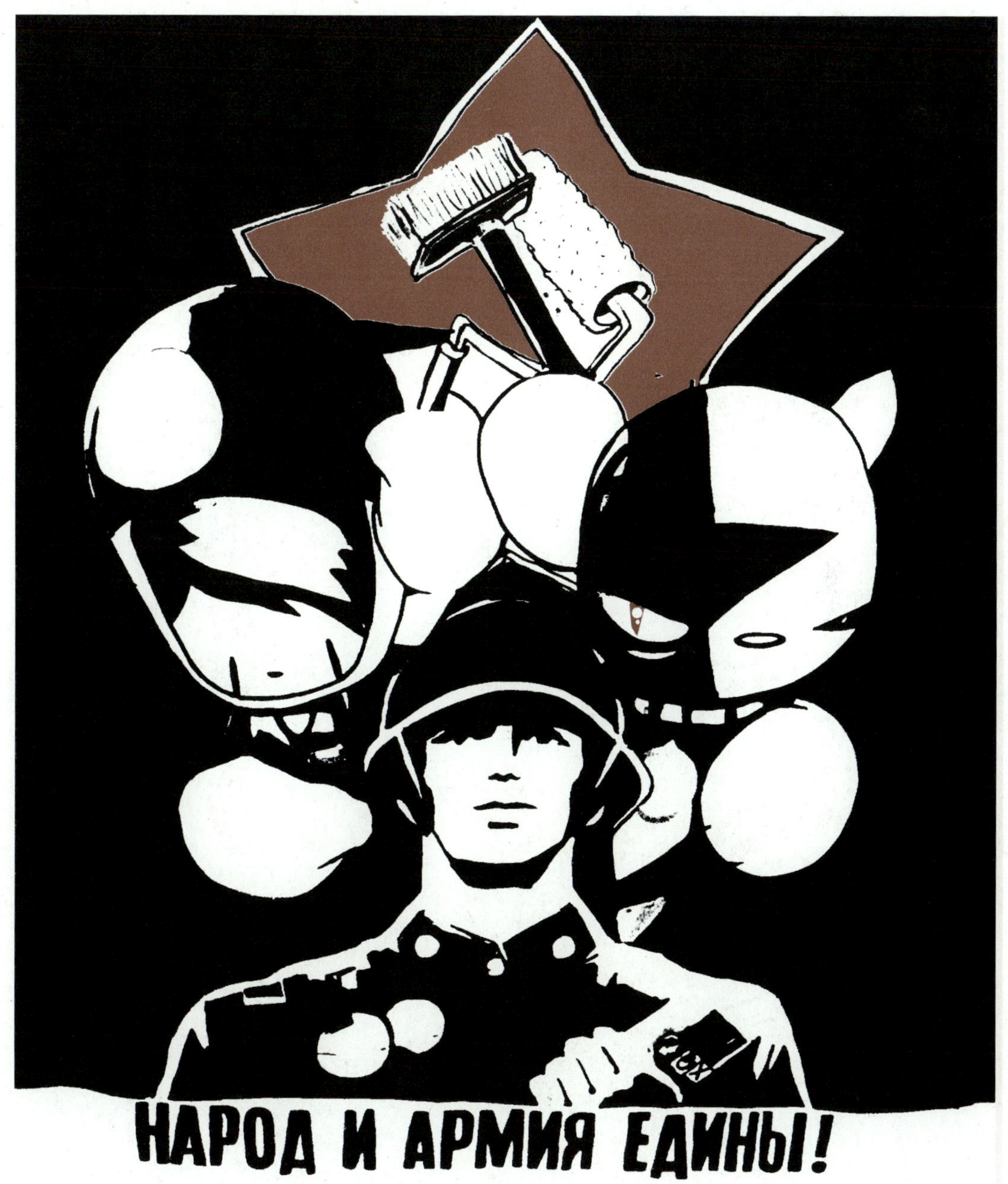

We started a revolution without weapons - mixed media on canvas - 100x80 cm - 2007

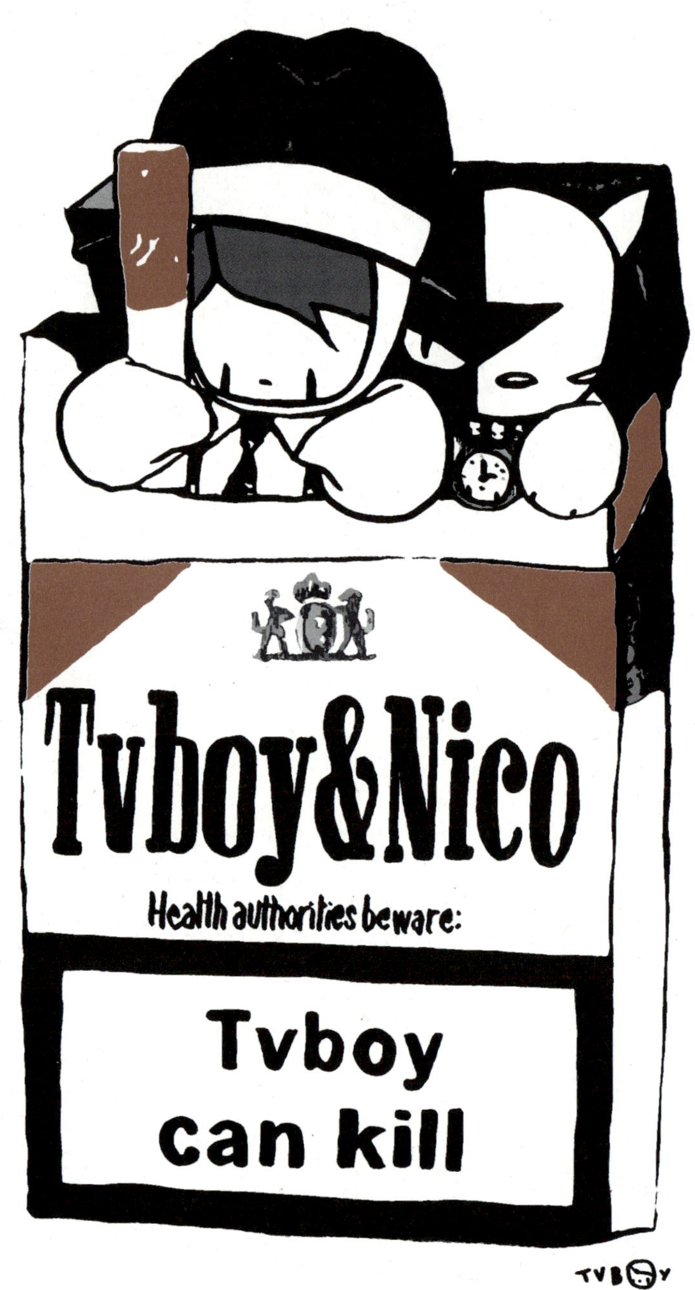

Marlboro - mixed media on canvas - 30x26 cm - 2007

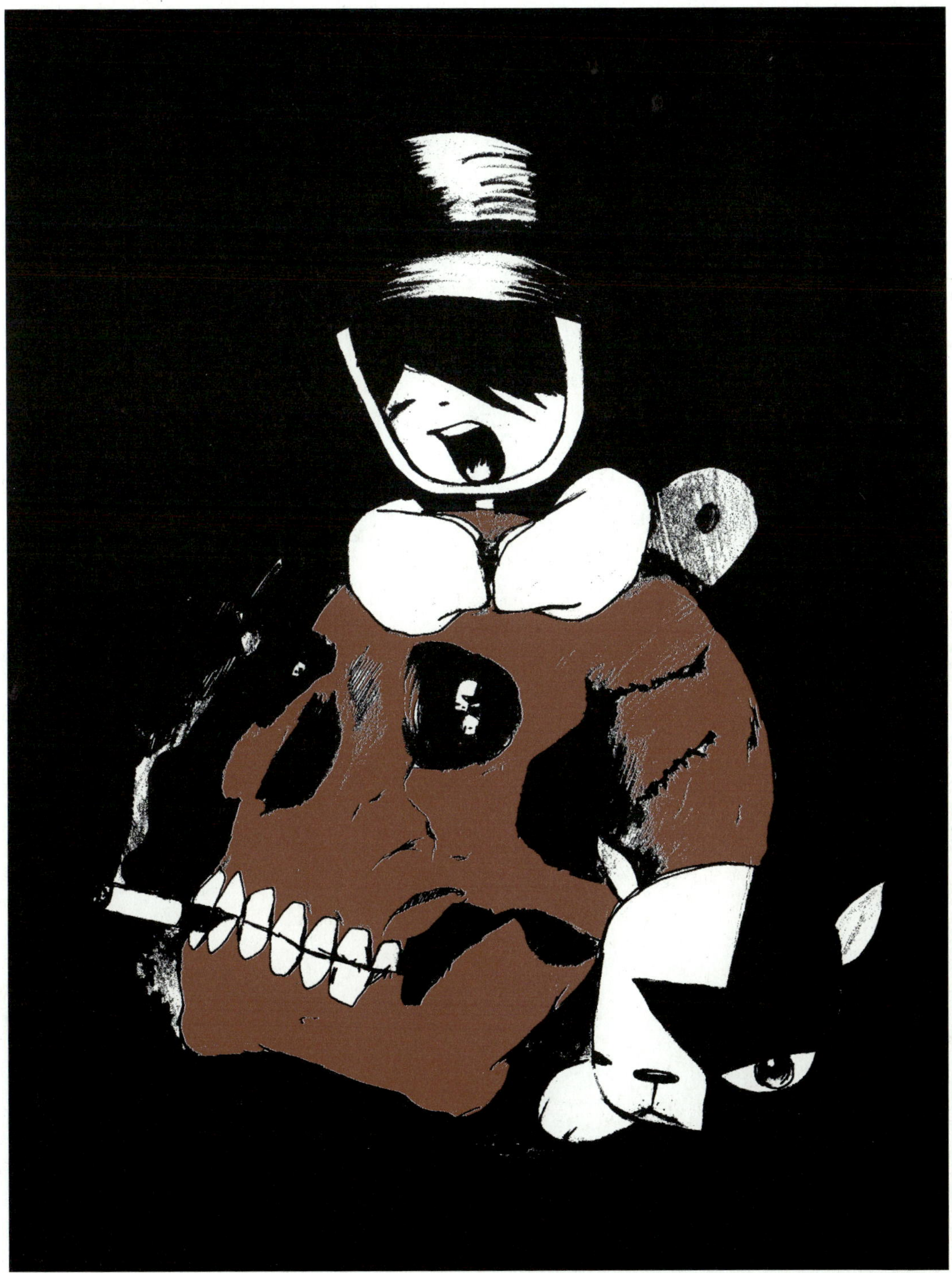

Death - mixed media on canvas - 40x30 cm - 2007

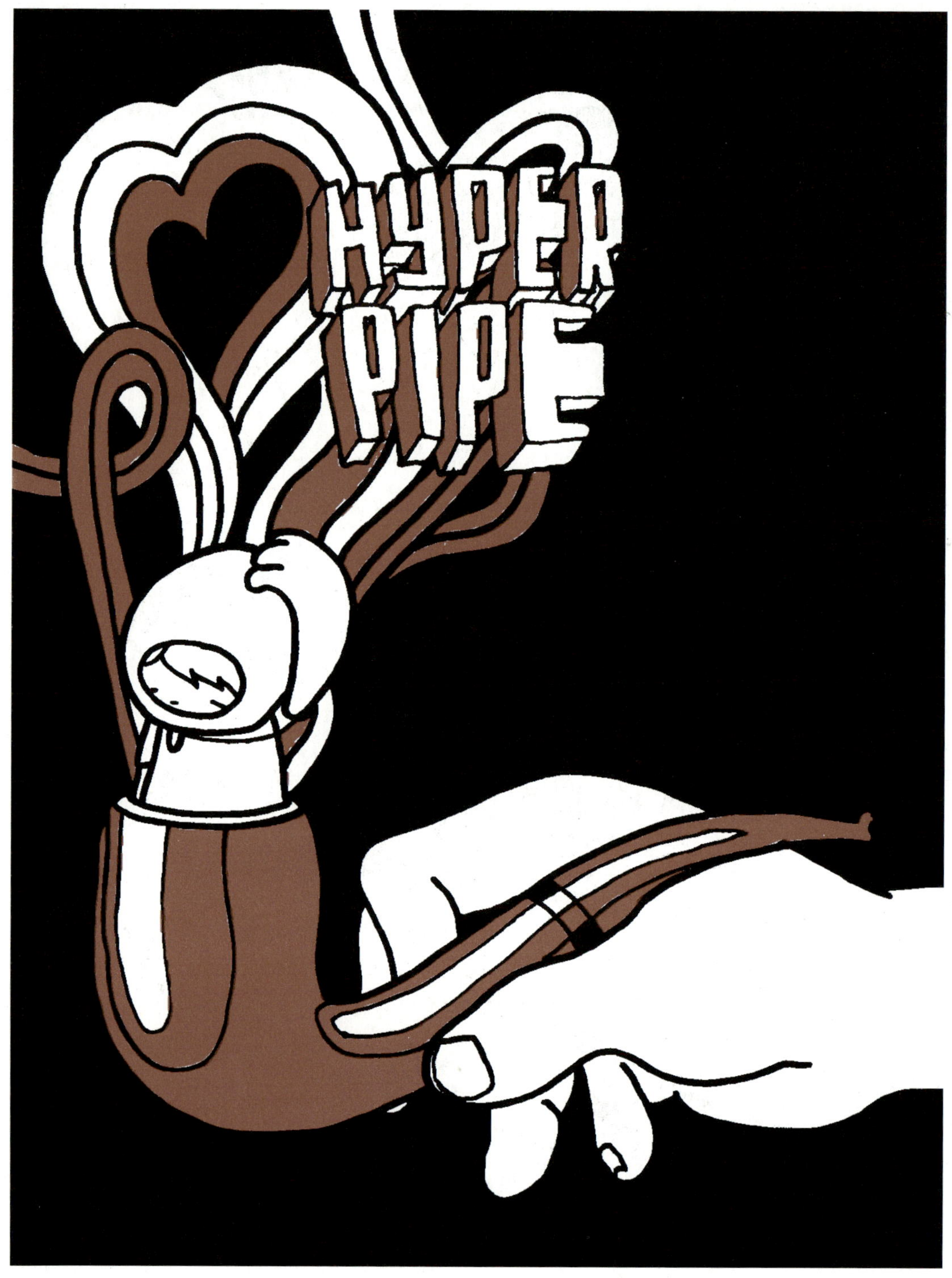

Hyper Pipe - Poster committed by Publicis for Hypegallery Campaign (Hp) - 2005

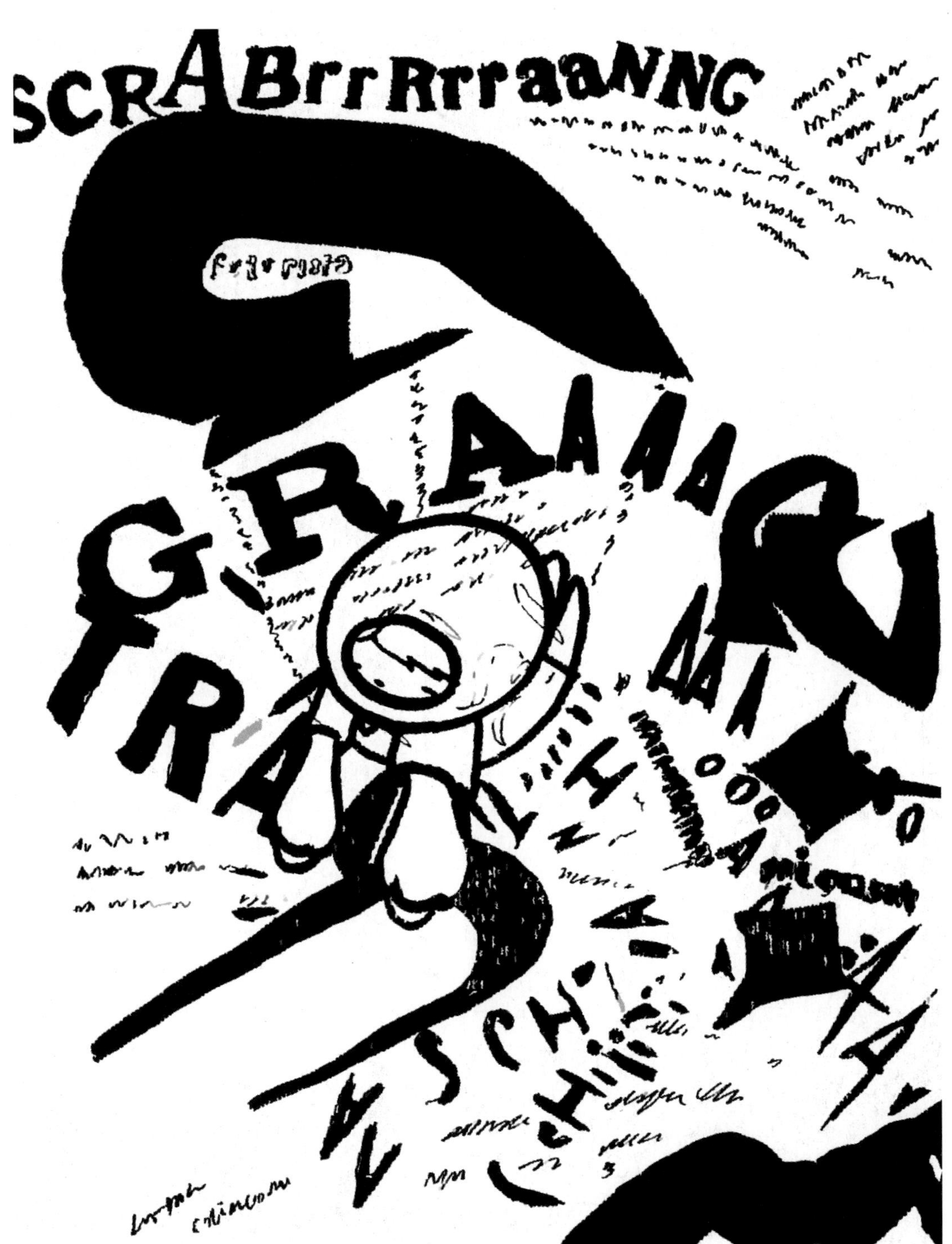

Paroliberismo - mixed media on canvas - 30x24 cm - 2005

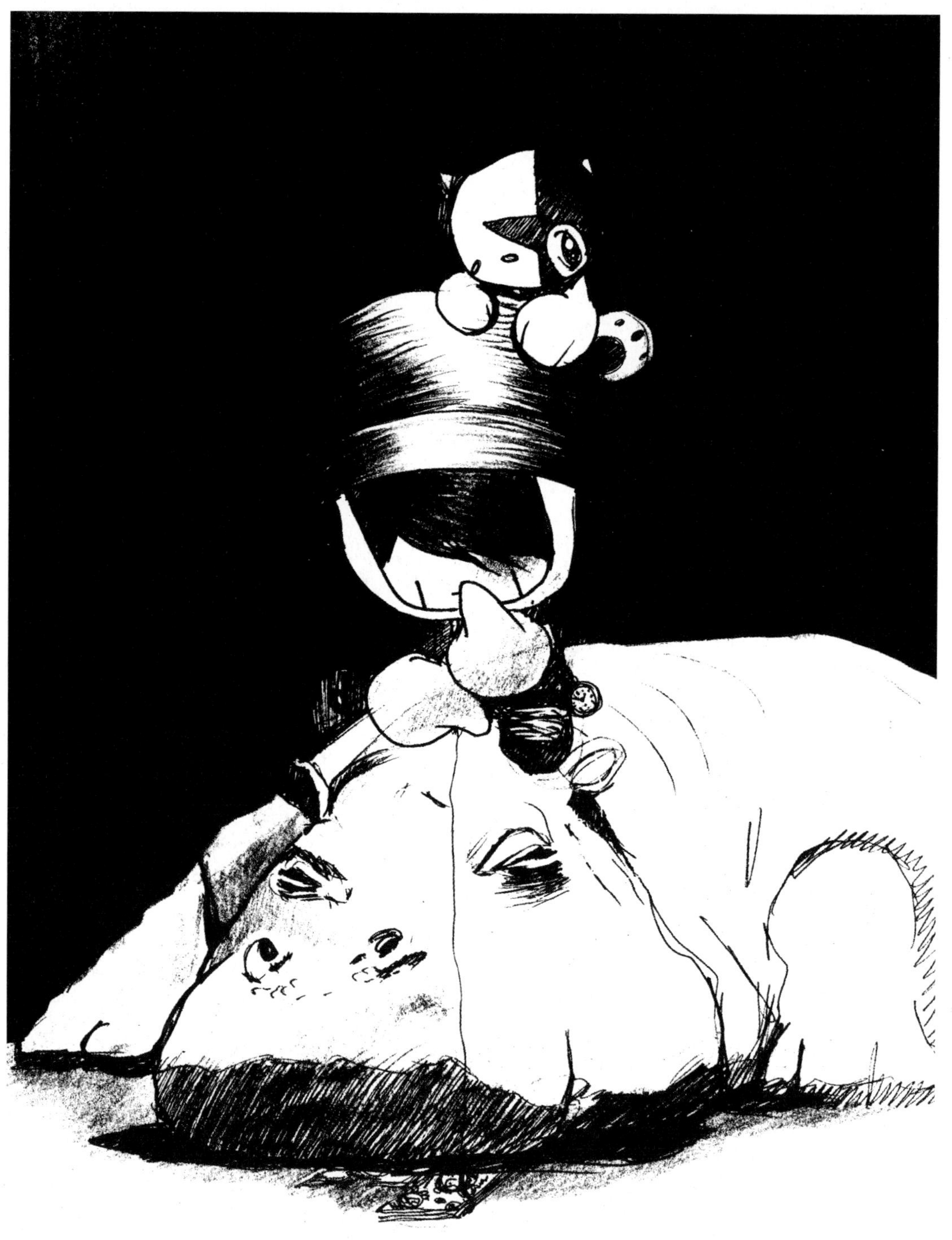

The Art of Making Money - ink on paper drawing - 40x30 cm - 2007

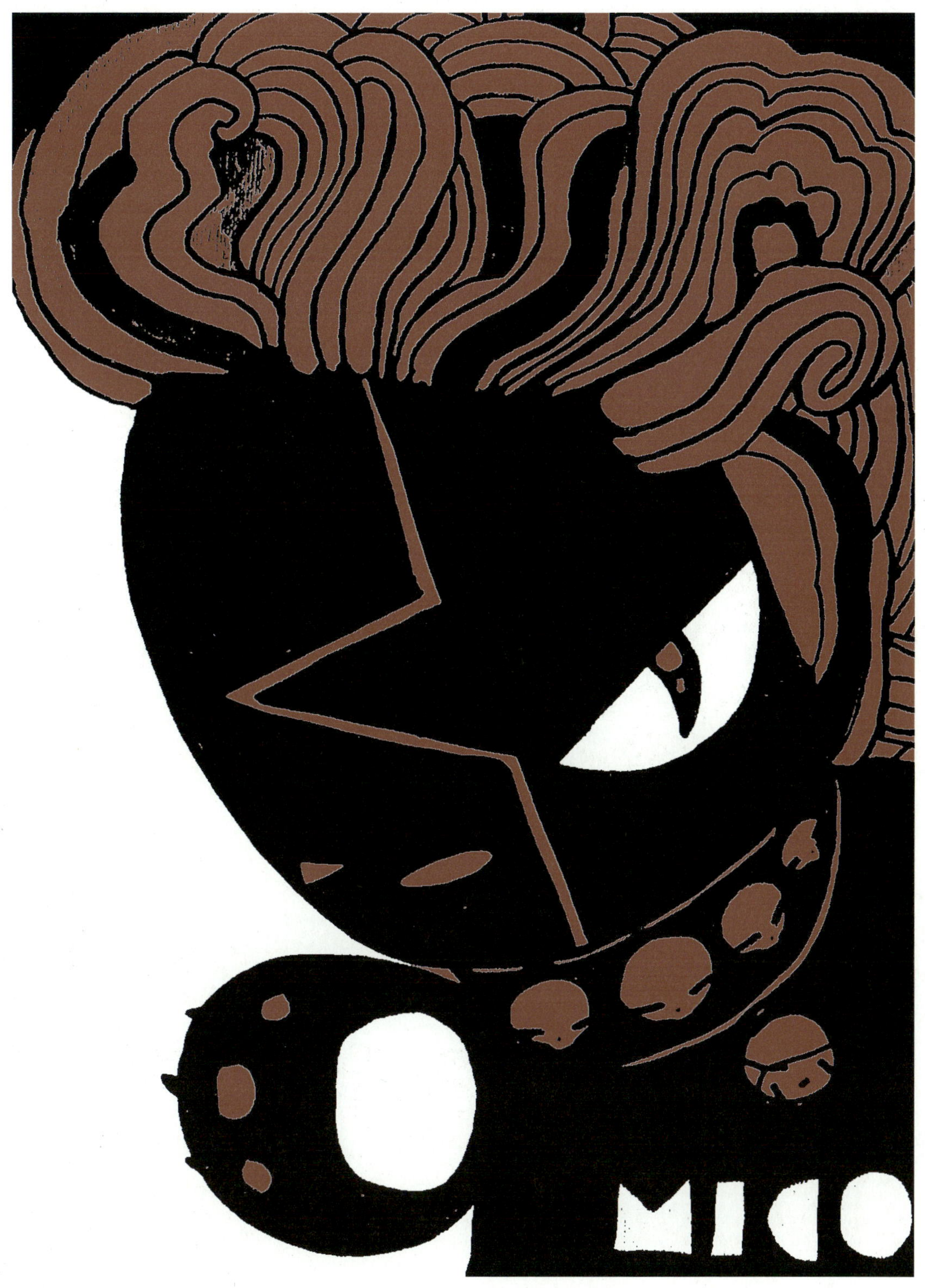

Dylan Dog - mixed media on canvas - 30x24 cm - 2007

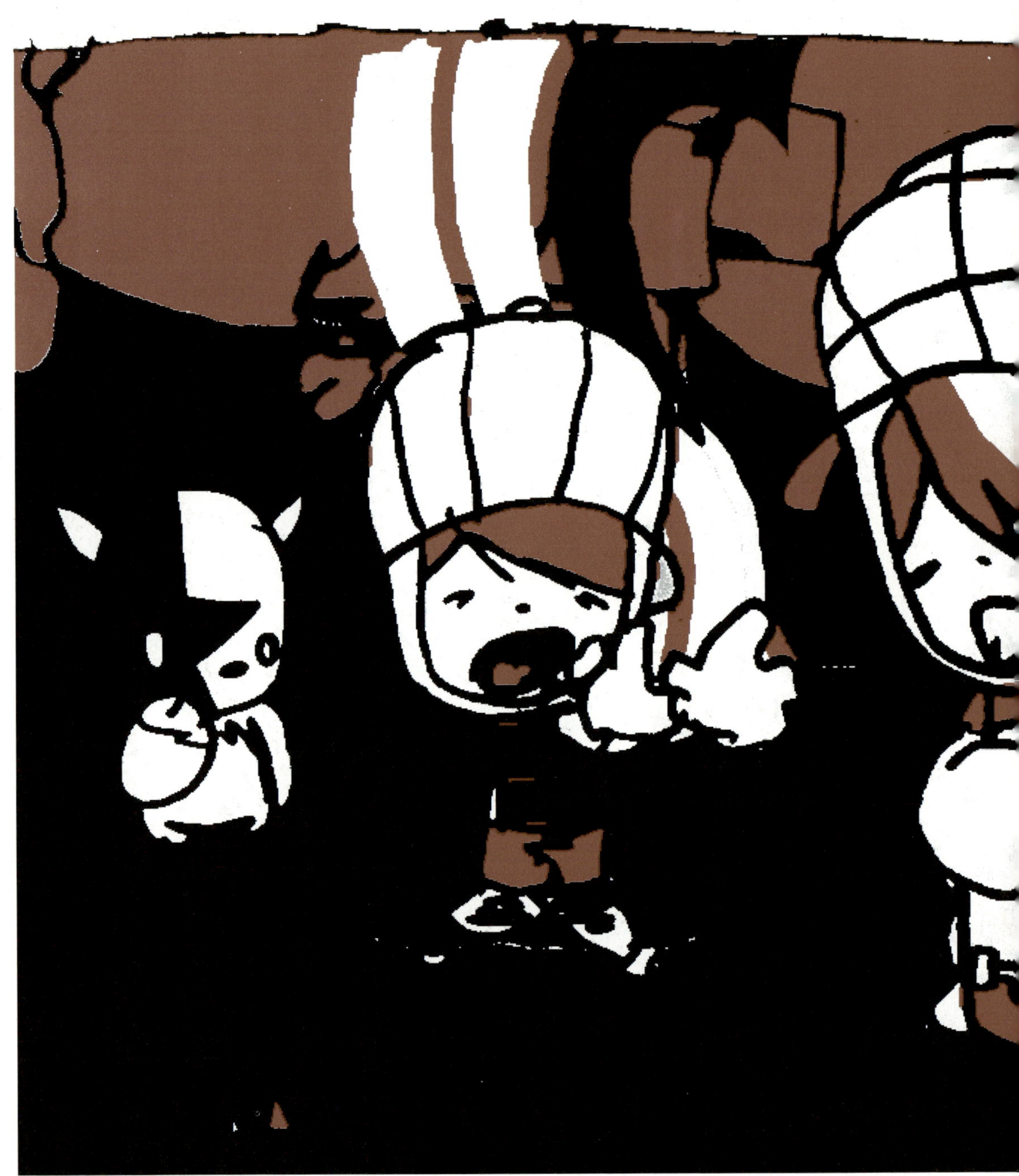

Scuole di strada - Illustration commited by Nescafé - 2007

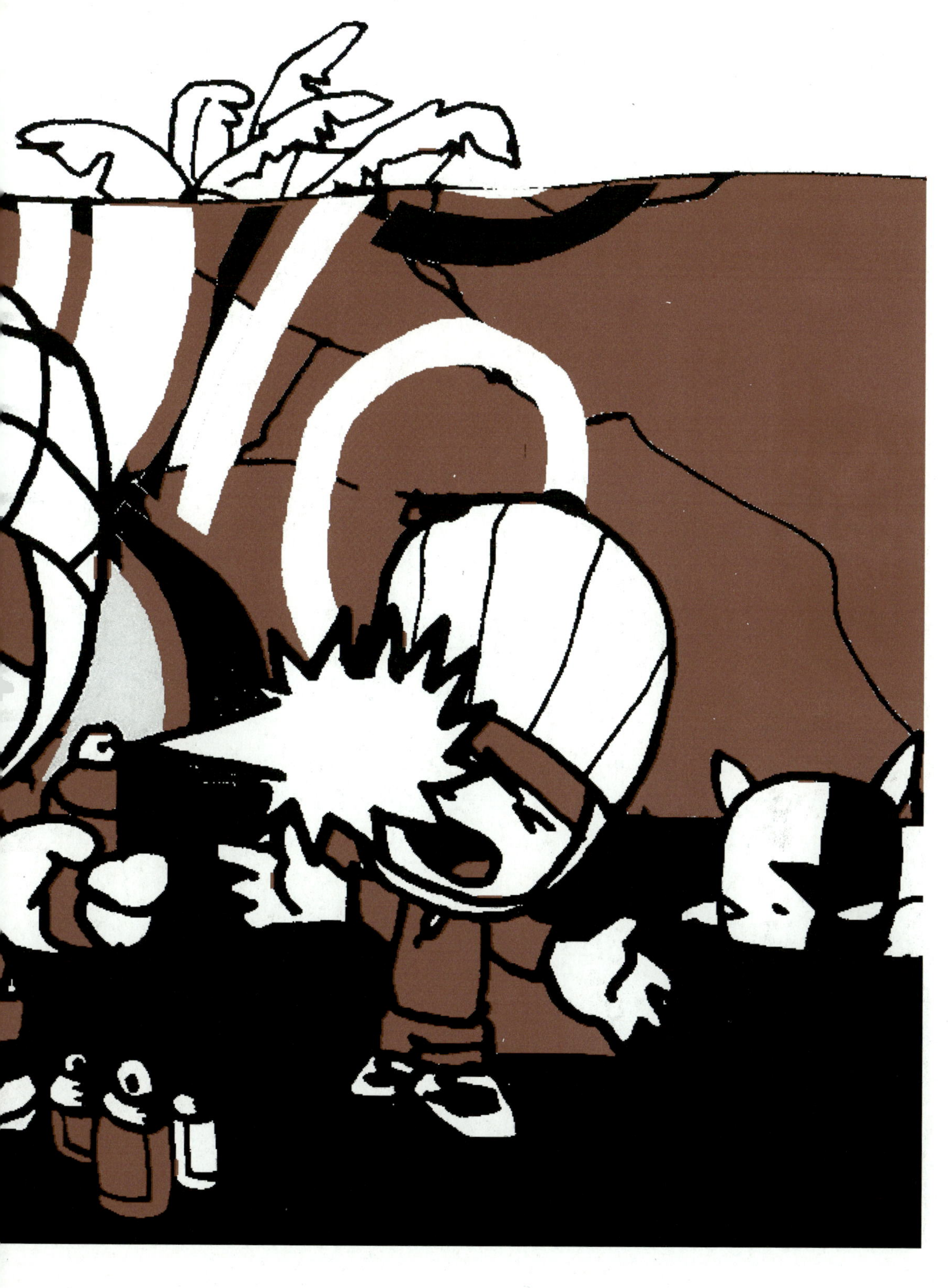

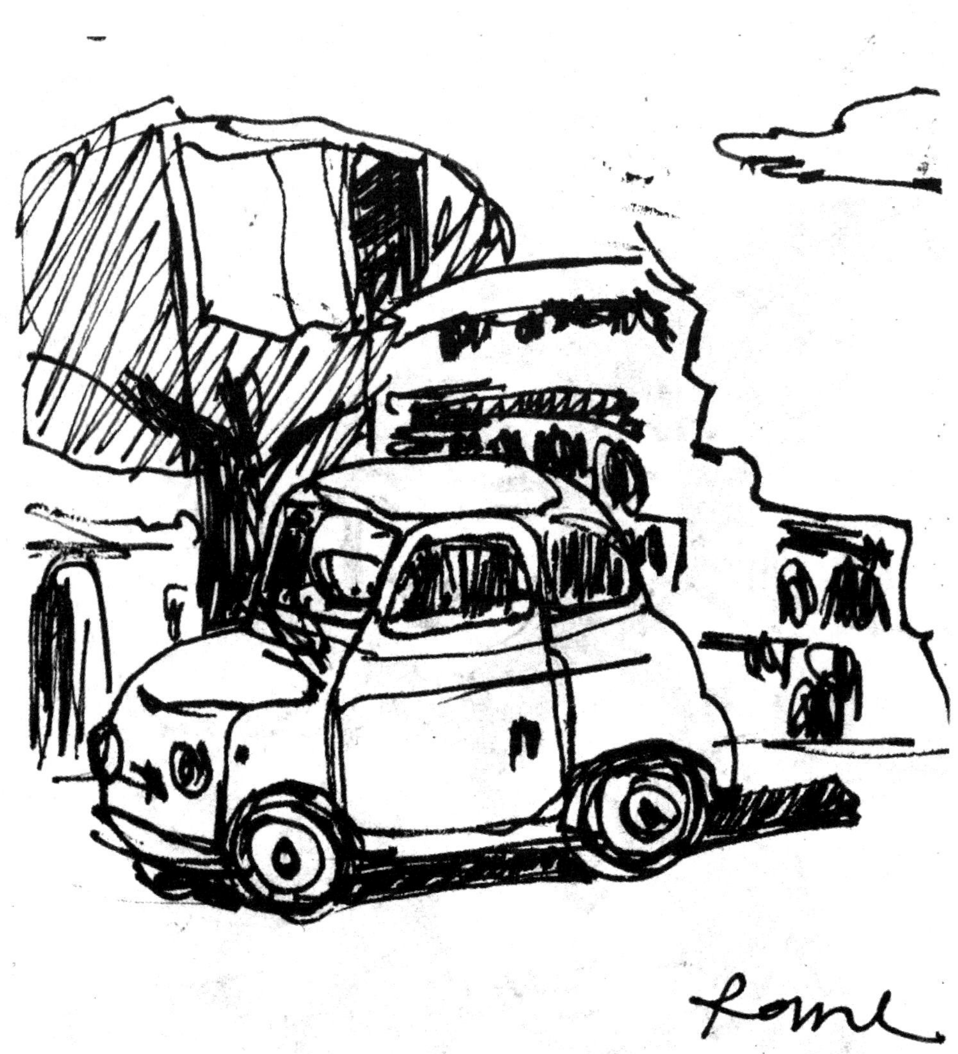

Roma - Ink on paper drawing - 40x30 cm - 2006

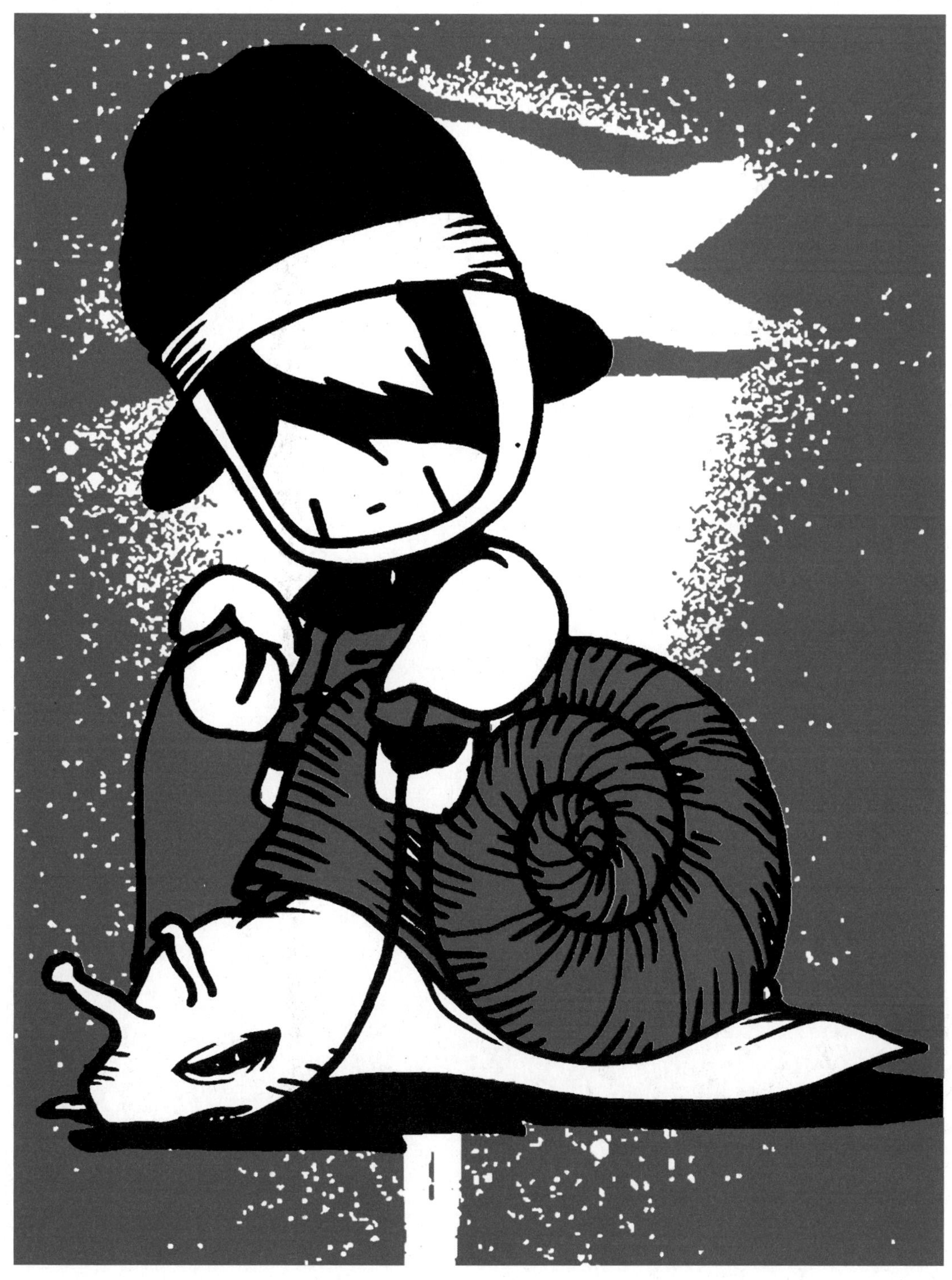

Slowly - ink on paper drawing - 40x30 cm - 2007

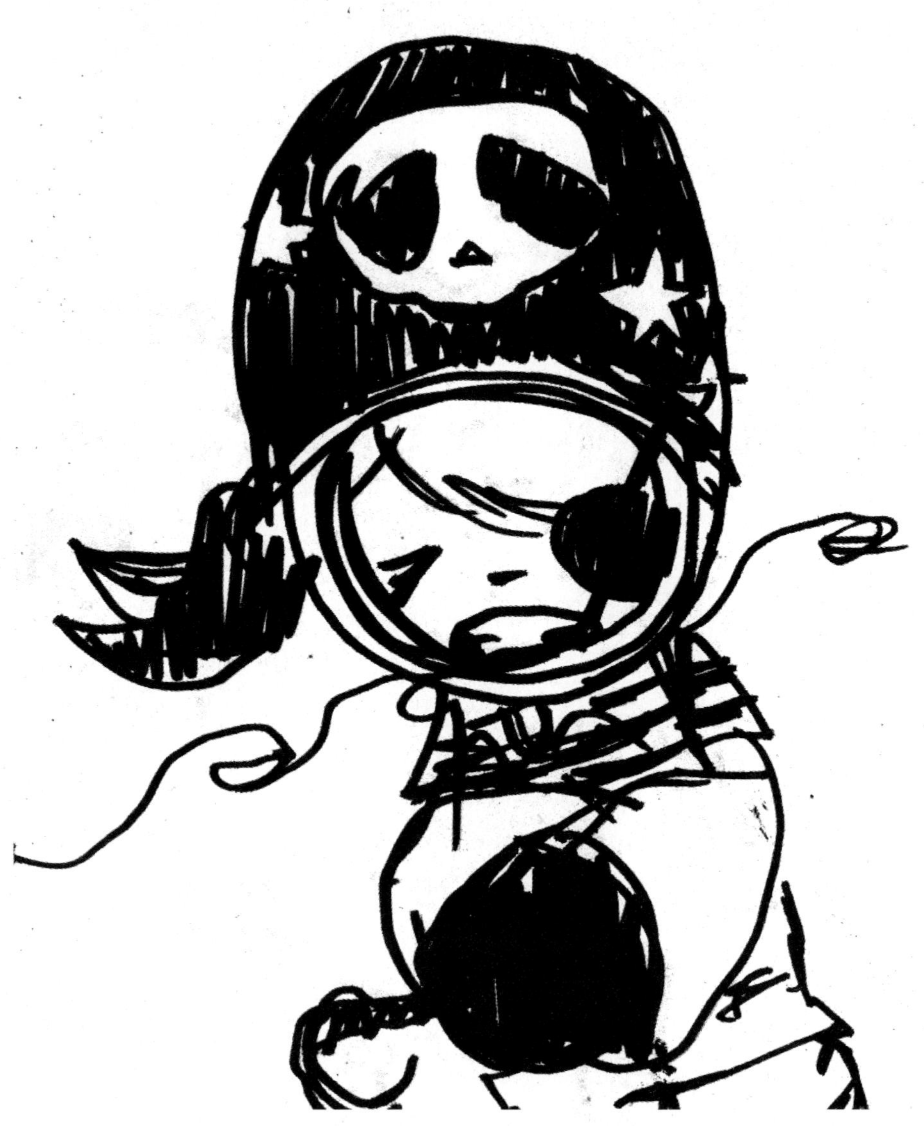

Pirate Boy - ink on paper sketch - 40x30 cm - 2006

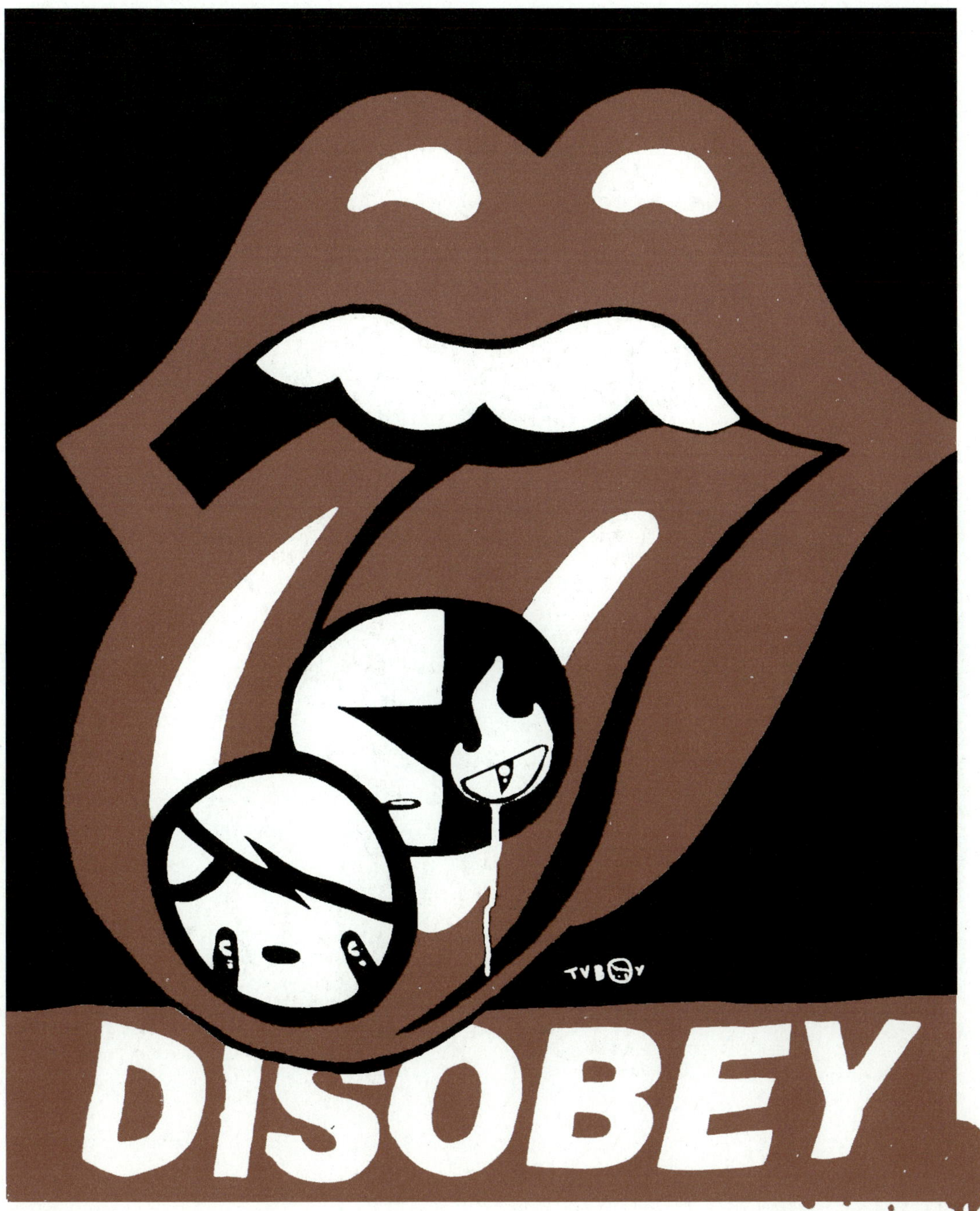

Disobey - mixed media on canvas - 100x80 cm - 2007

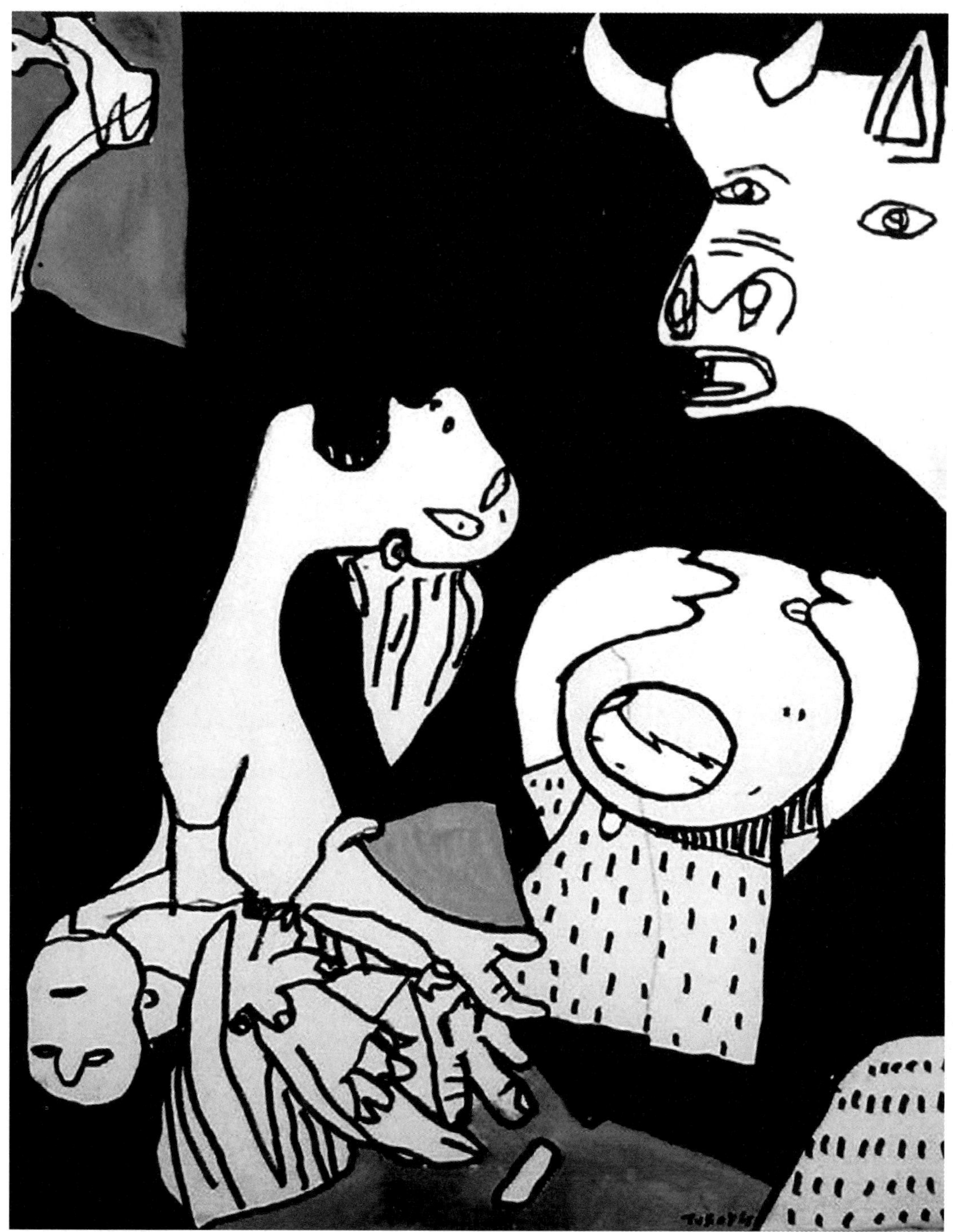

Guernica - mixed media on canvas - 30x24 cm - 2005

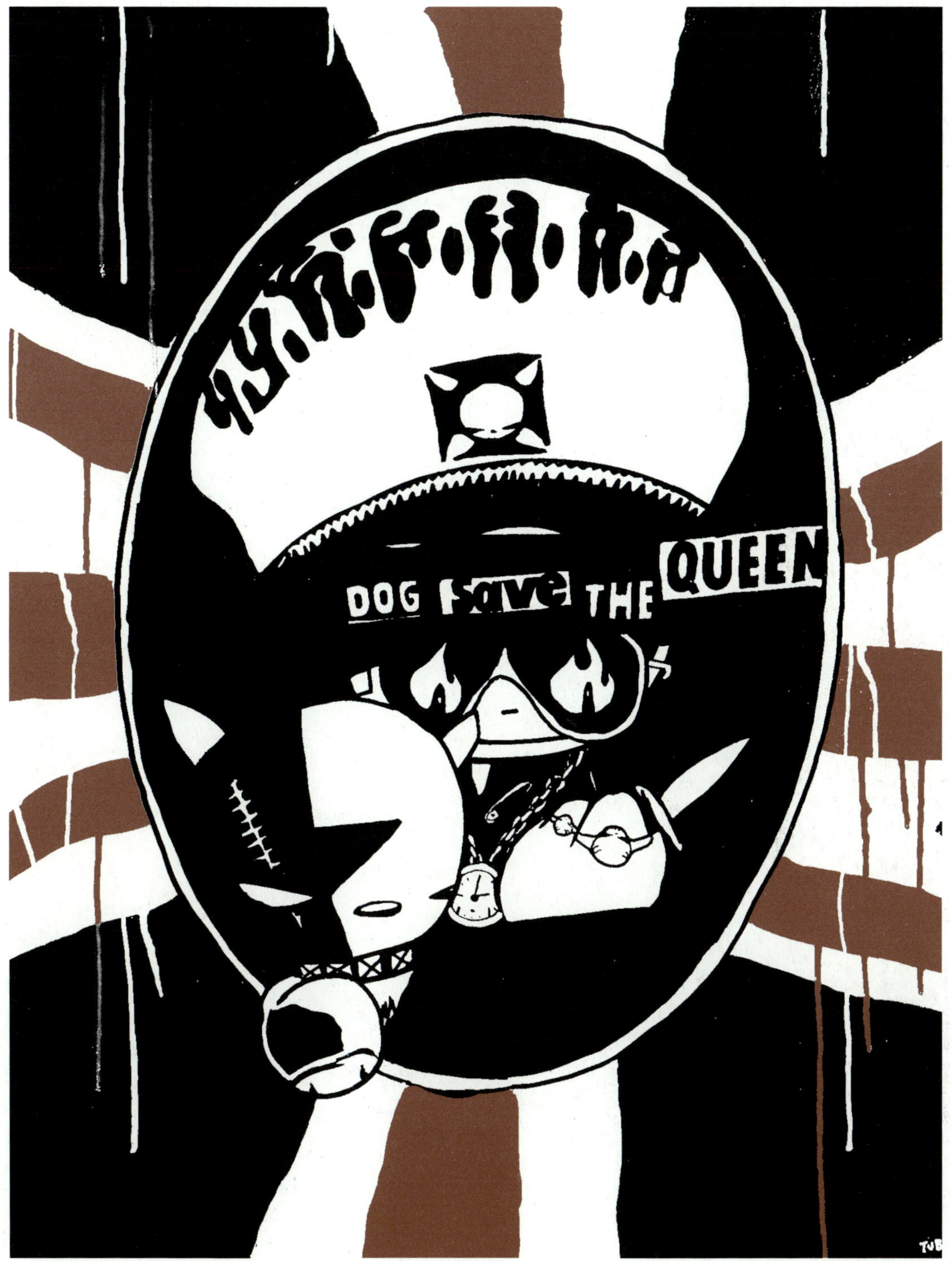

Dog Save the Queen - mixed media on canvas - 70x63 cm - 2007

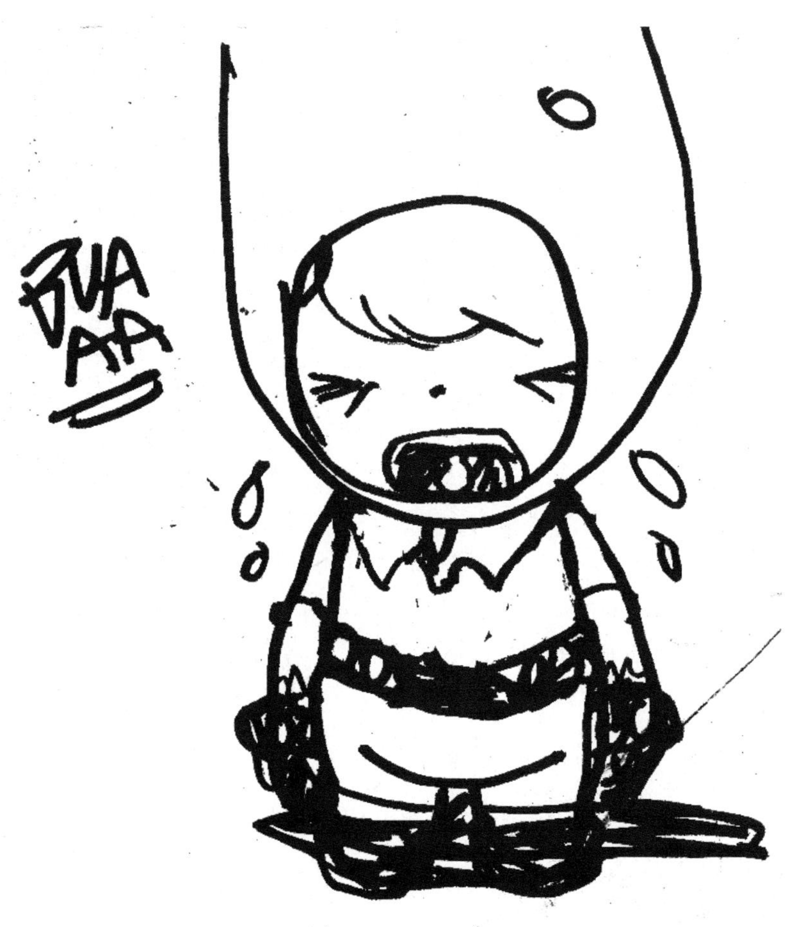

Buaaa - ink on paper sketch - 40x30 cm - 2006

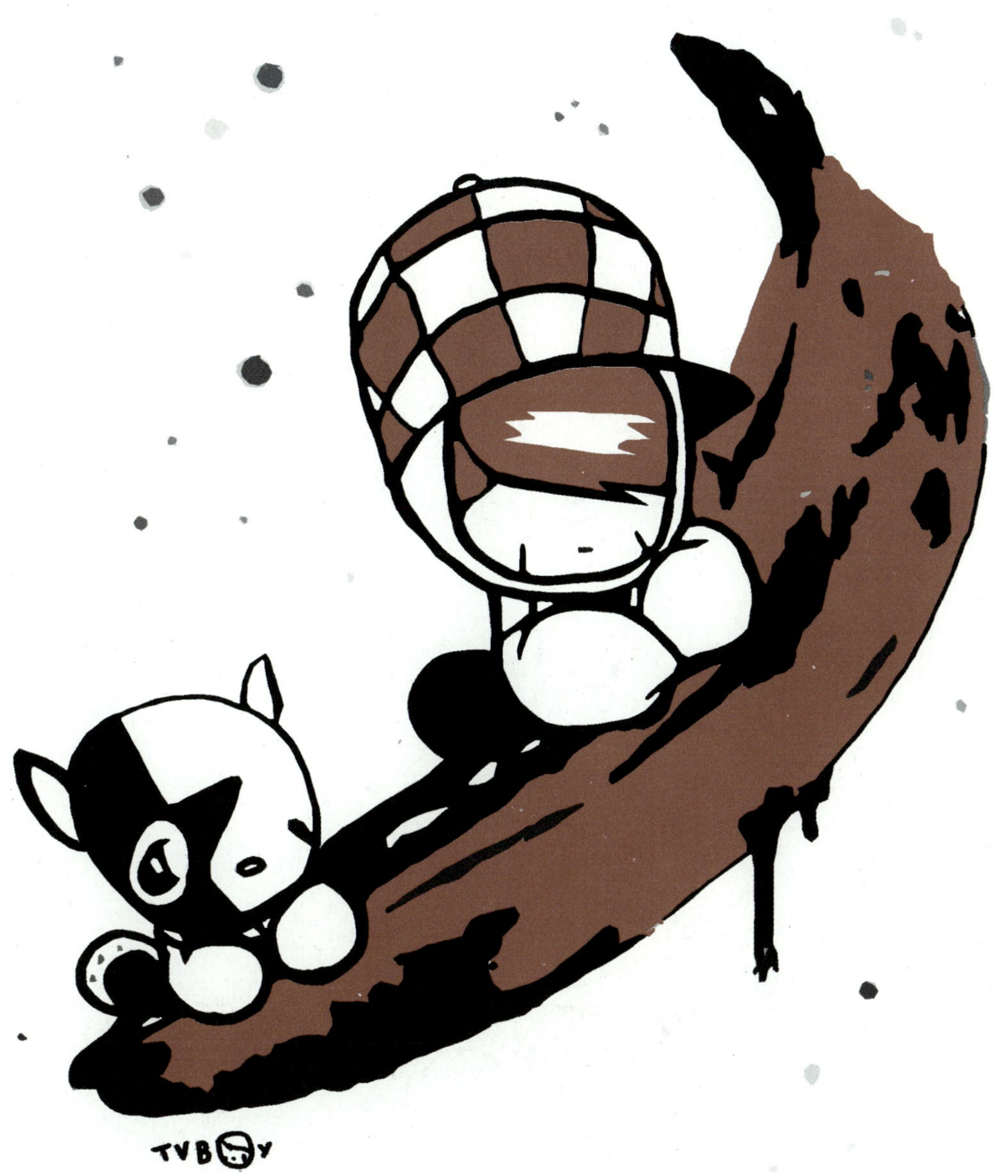

Banana - mixed media on canvas - 100x80 cm - 2007

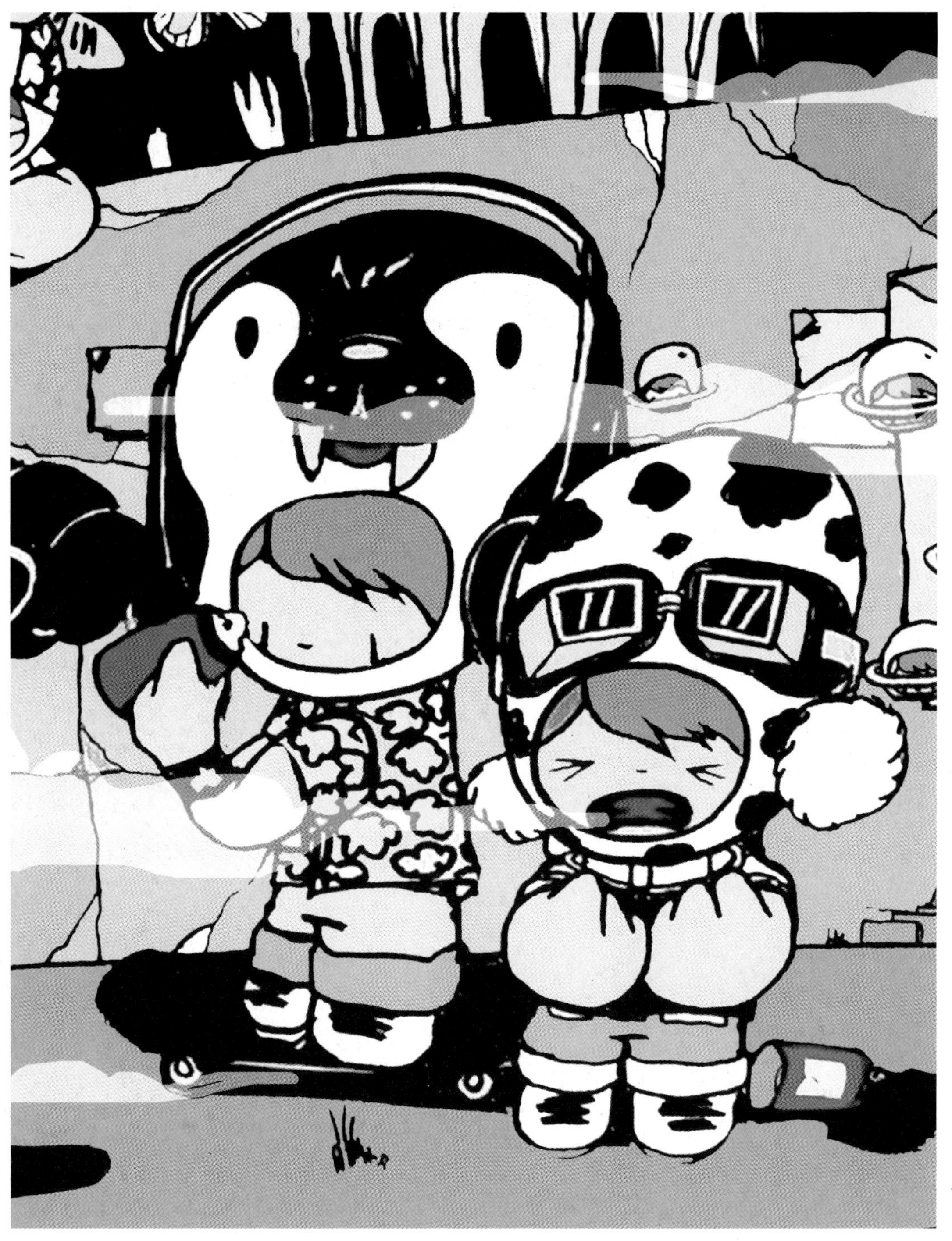

Love in Pisa (detail) - Mixed media on canvas - 100x80 cm - 2006

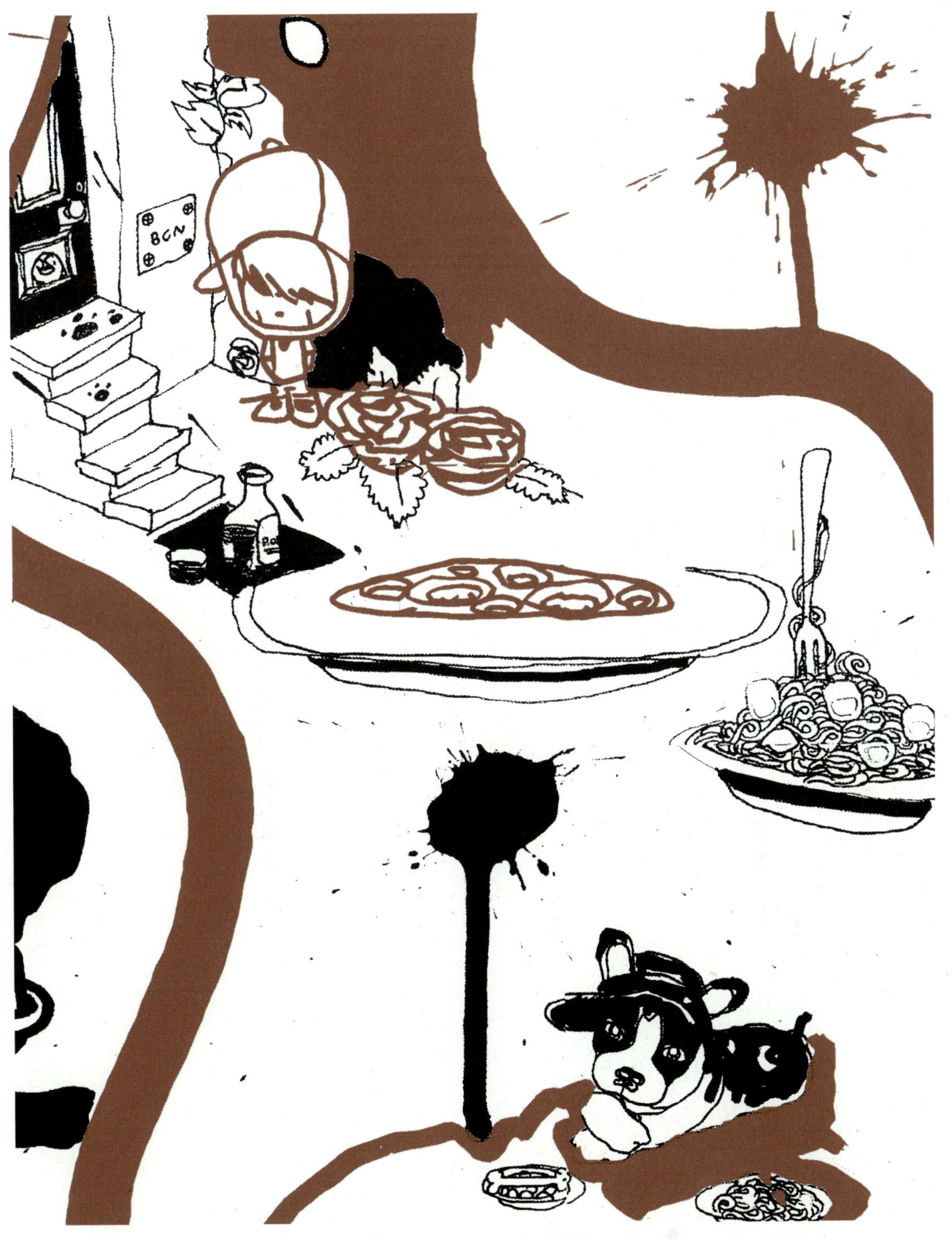

Illustration for Studenti Mediagroup - **markers on canvas -2006**

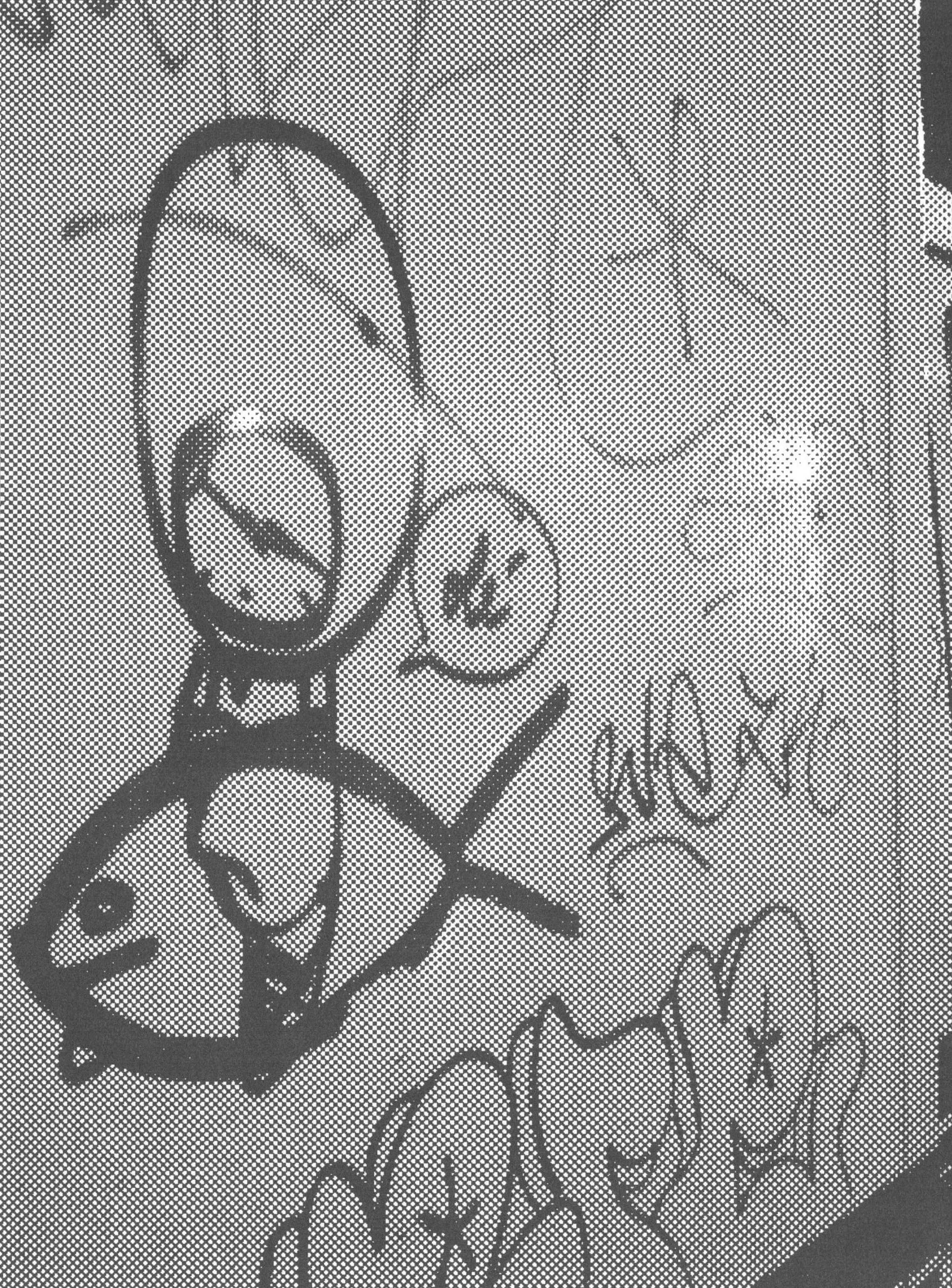

GRAFFITI

Start a Revolution without Weapons

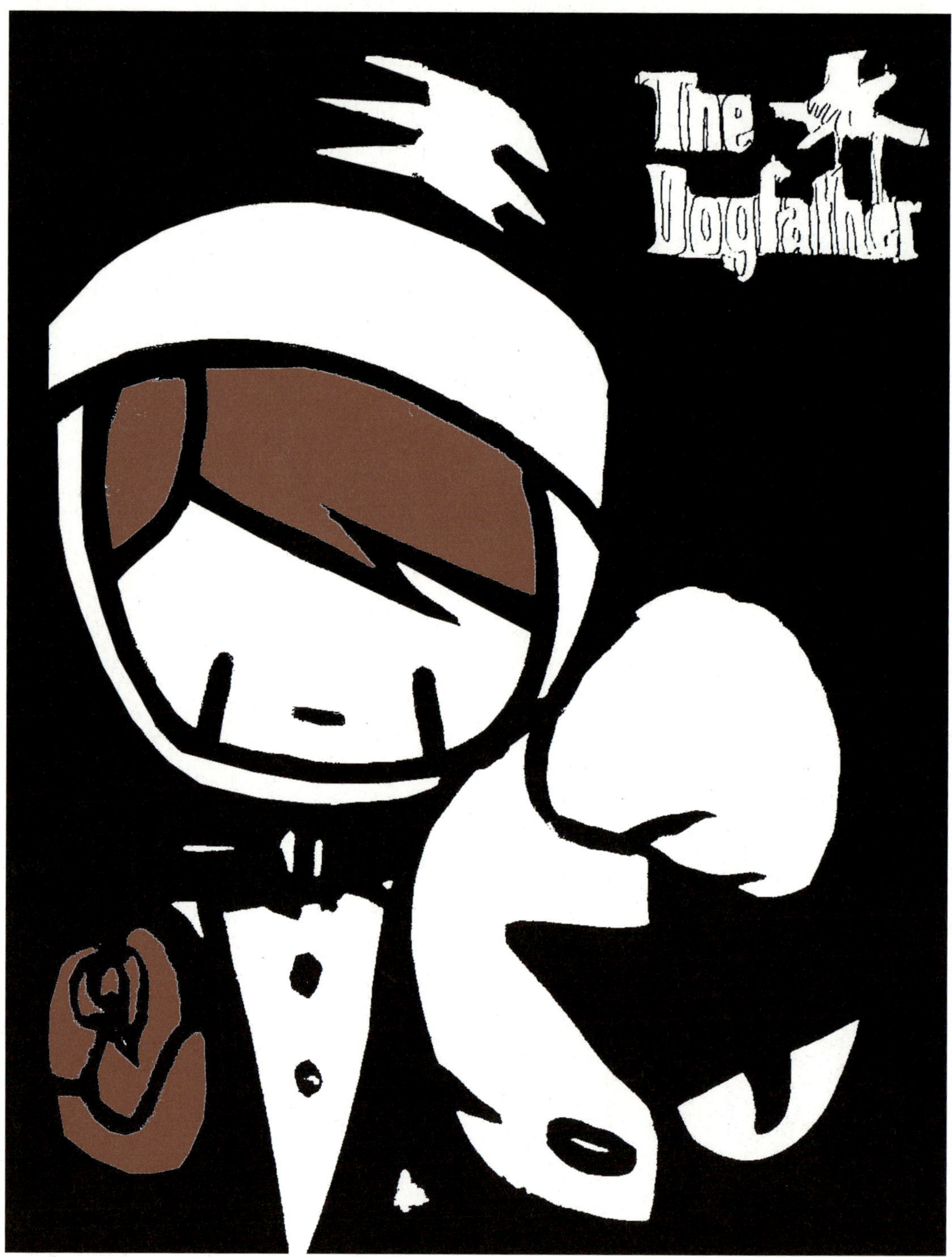

The Dog Father mixed media on paper - 2007

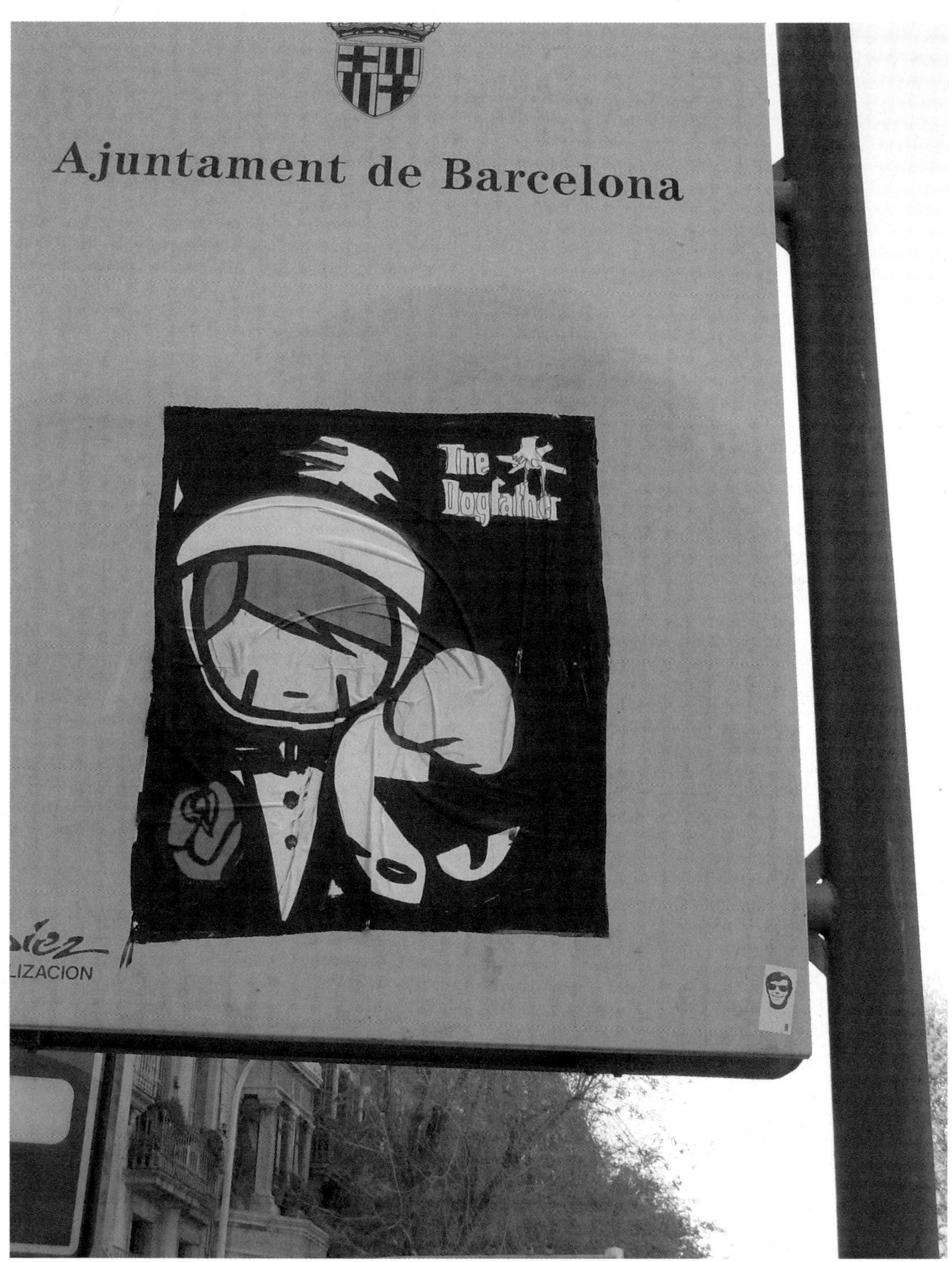

The Dog Father   wheat pasted poster - Barcelona - 2007

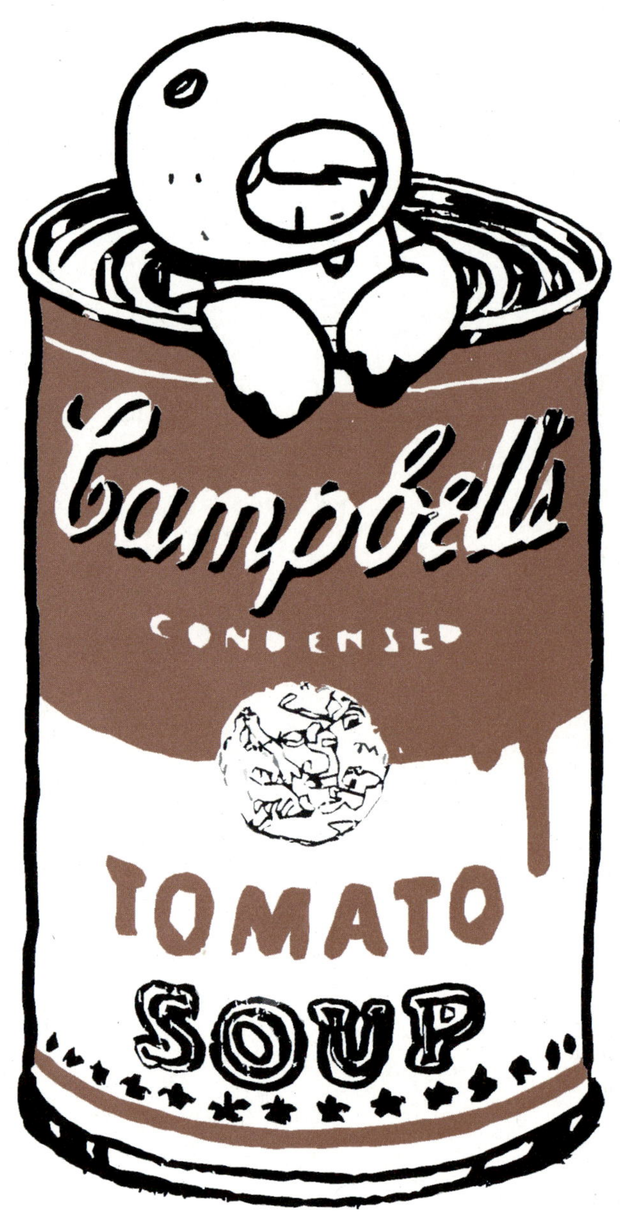

Campbell Soup mixed media on canvas - 23x30 cm - 2004

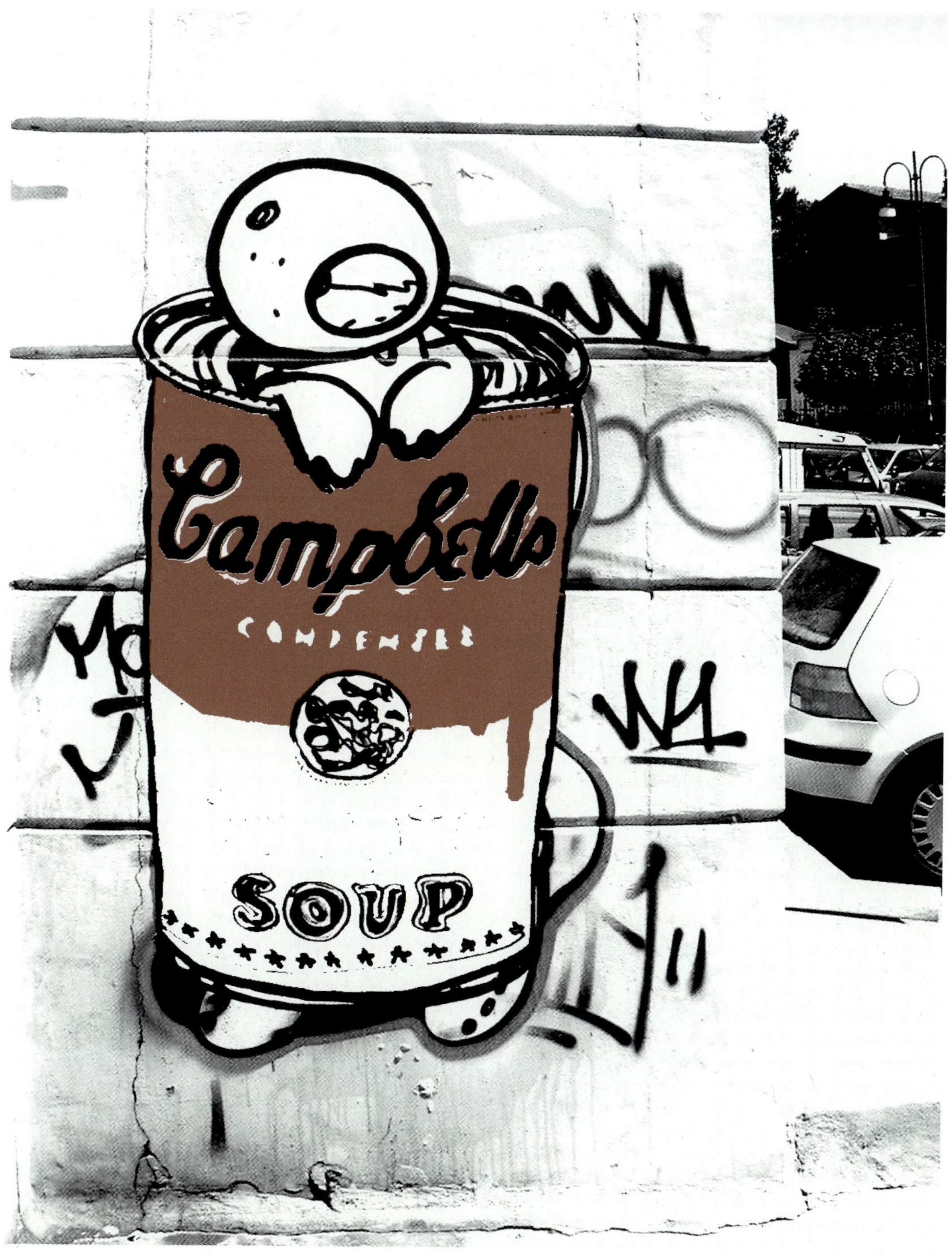

Campbell Soup wheat pasted poster - Milano - 2004

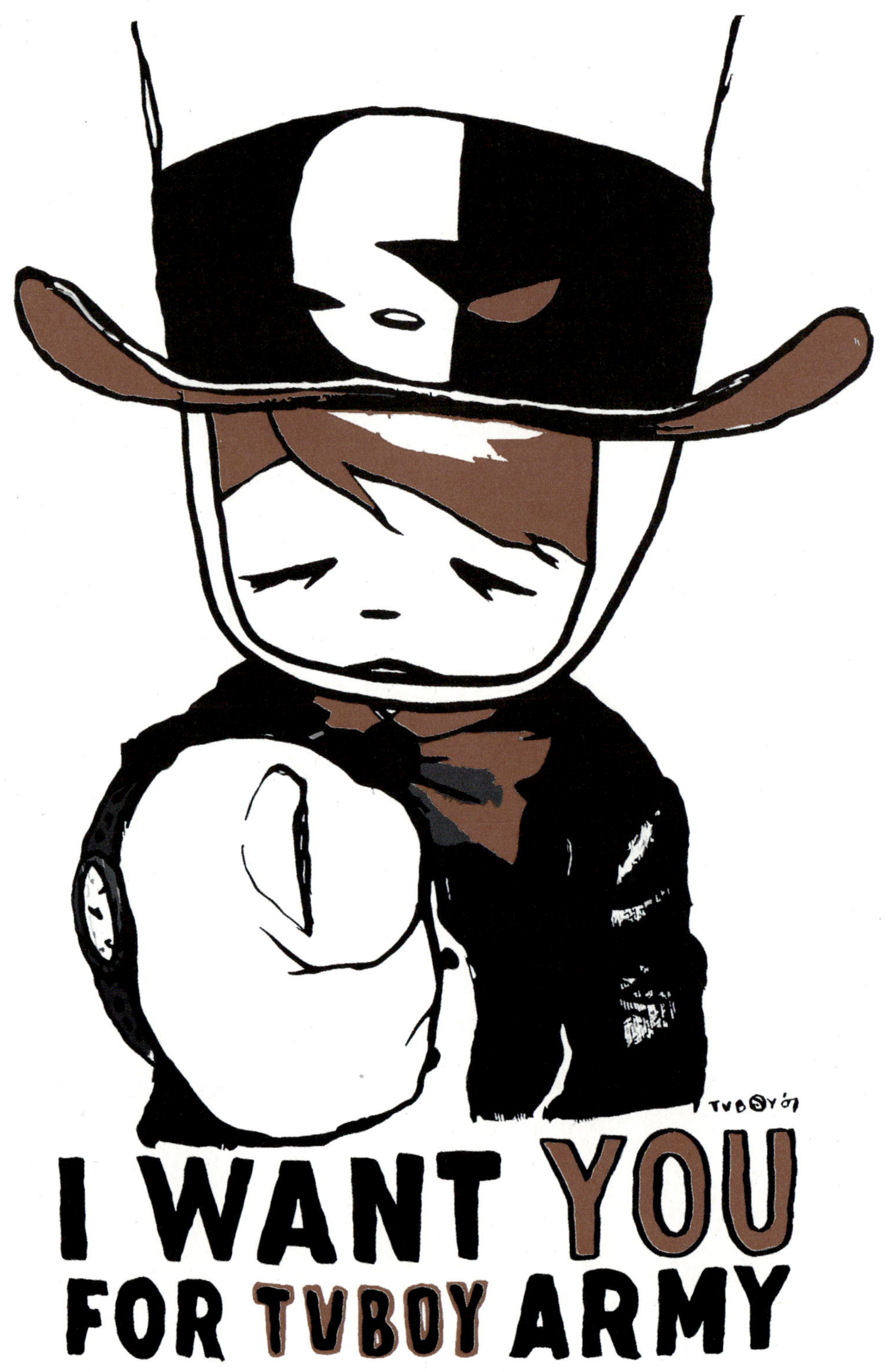

Uncle Sam mixed media on canvas - 26x30 cm - 2007

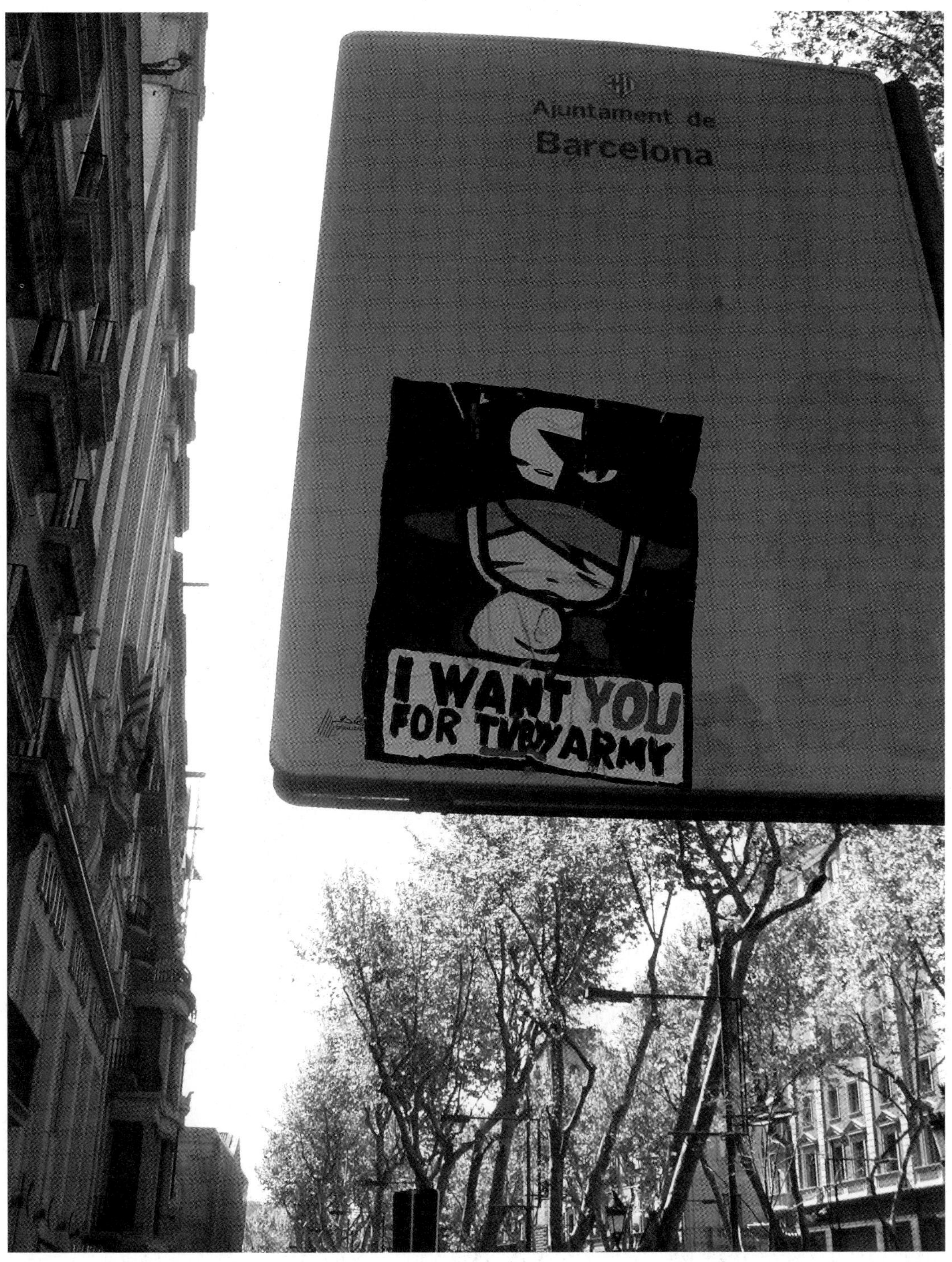

Uncle Sam wheat pasted poster - Barcelona - 2007

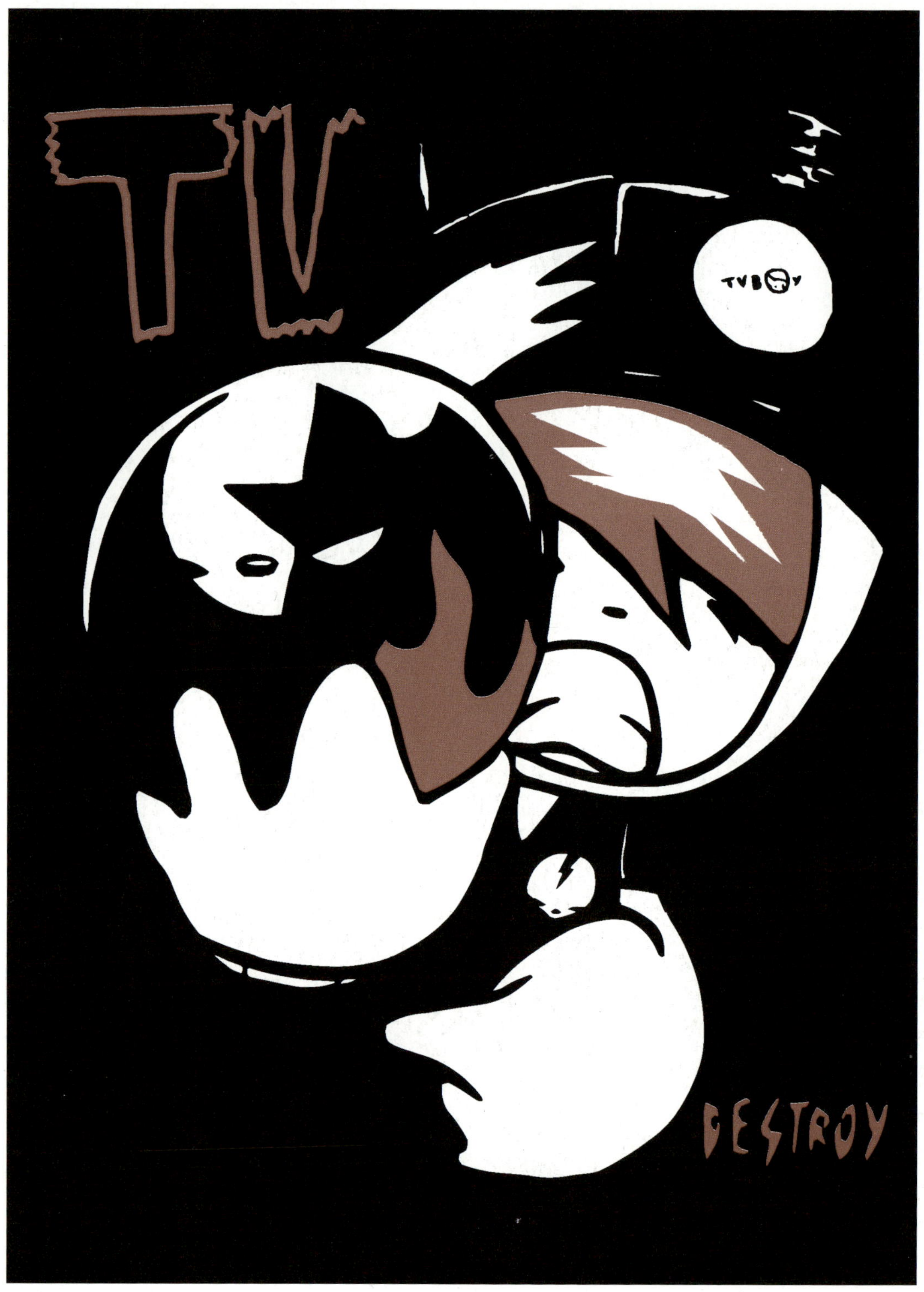

Tv Destroy mixed media on canvas - 80x100 cm - 2007

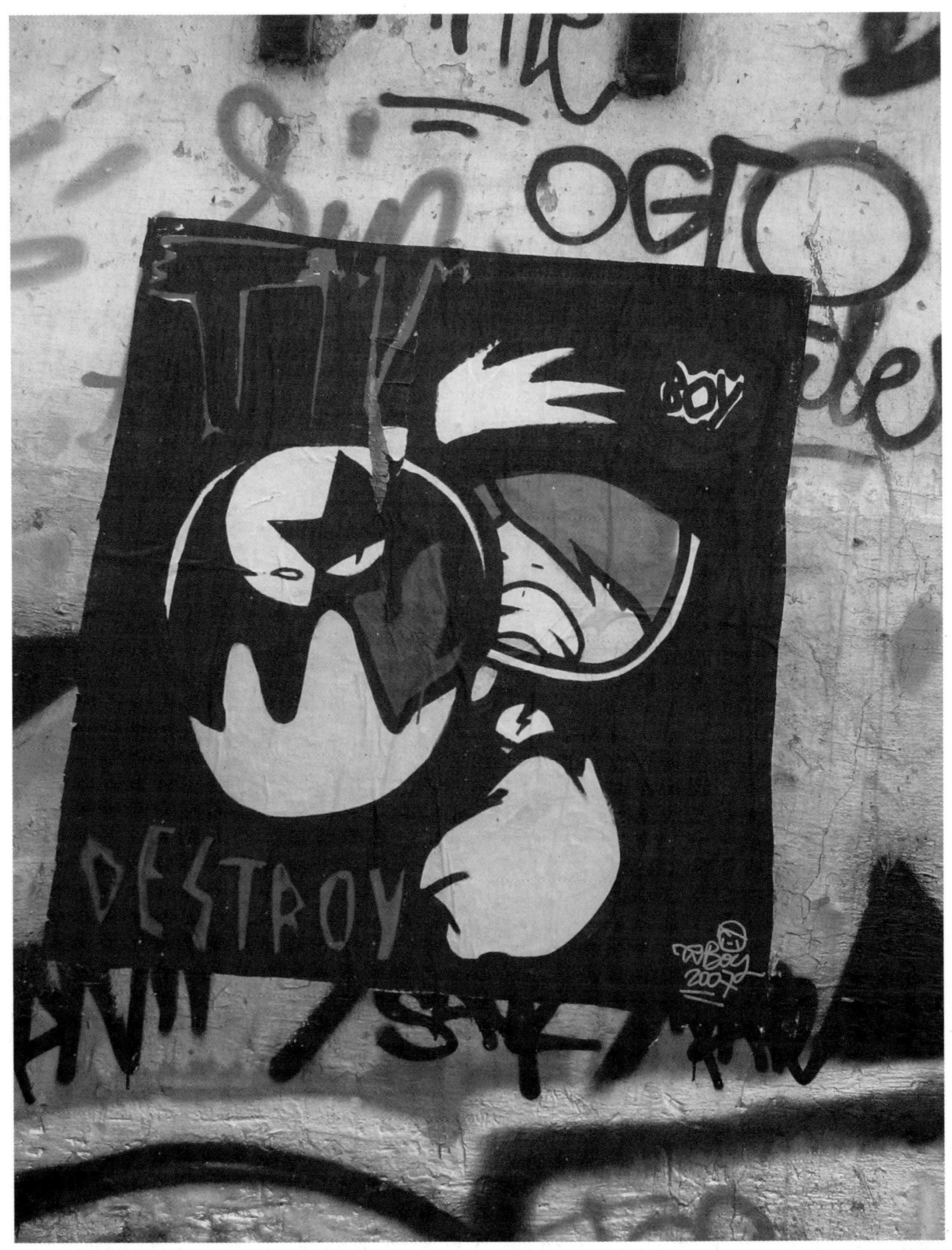

Tv Destroy wheat pasted poster - Barcelona - 2007

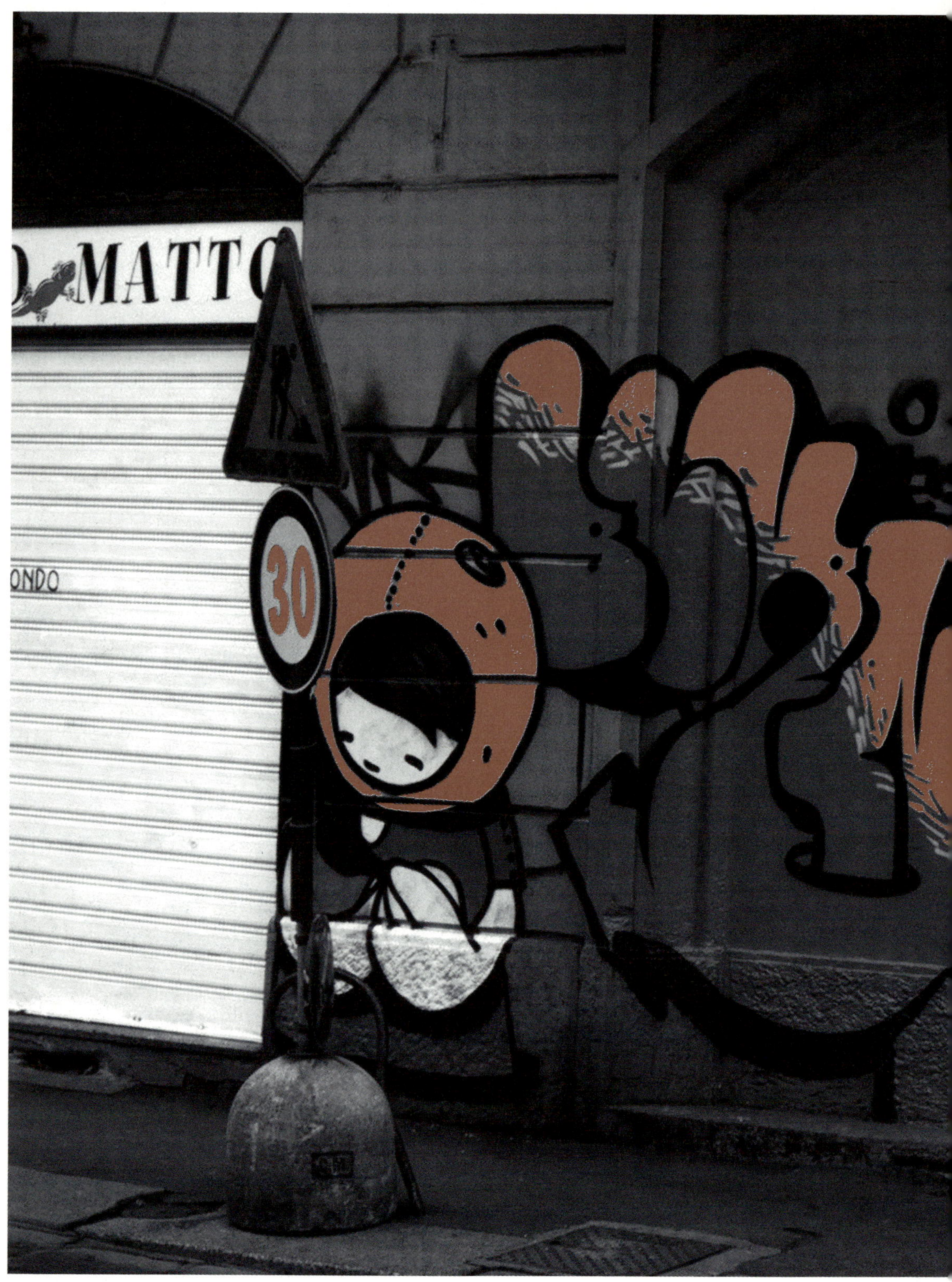

Illegal graff with Flying Fortress, Burns, Ivan - Milano - 2005

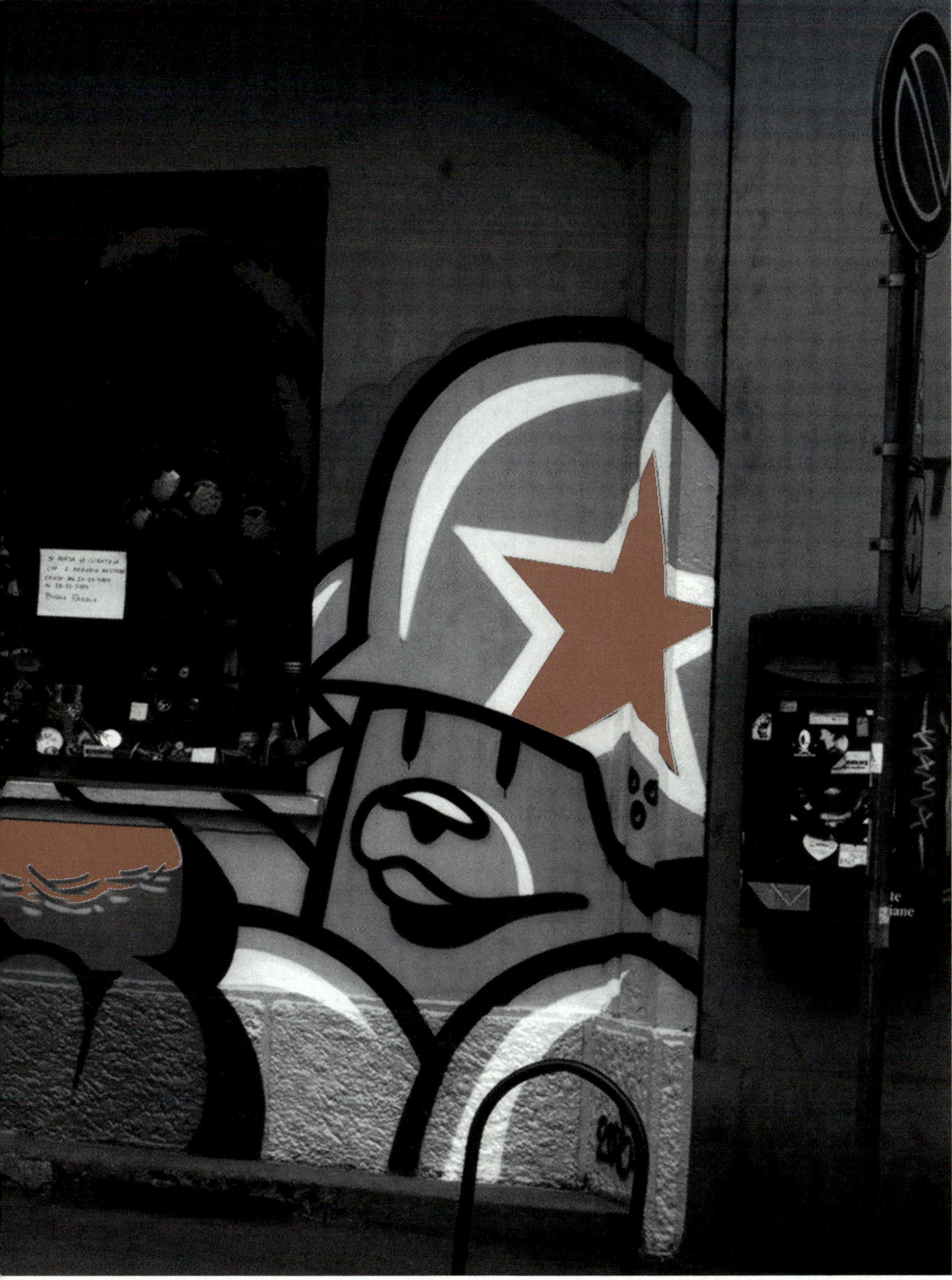

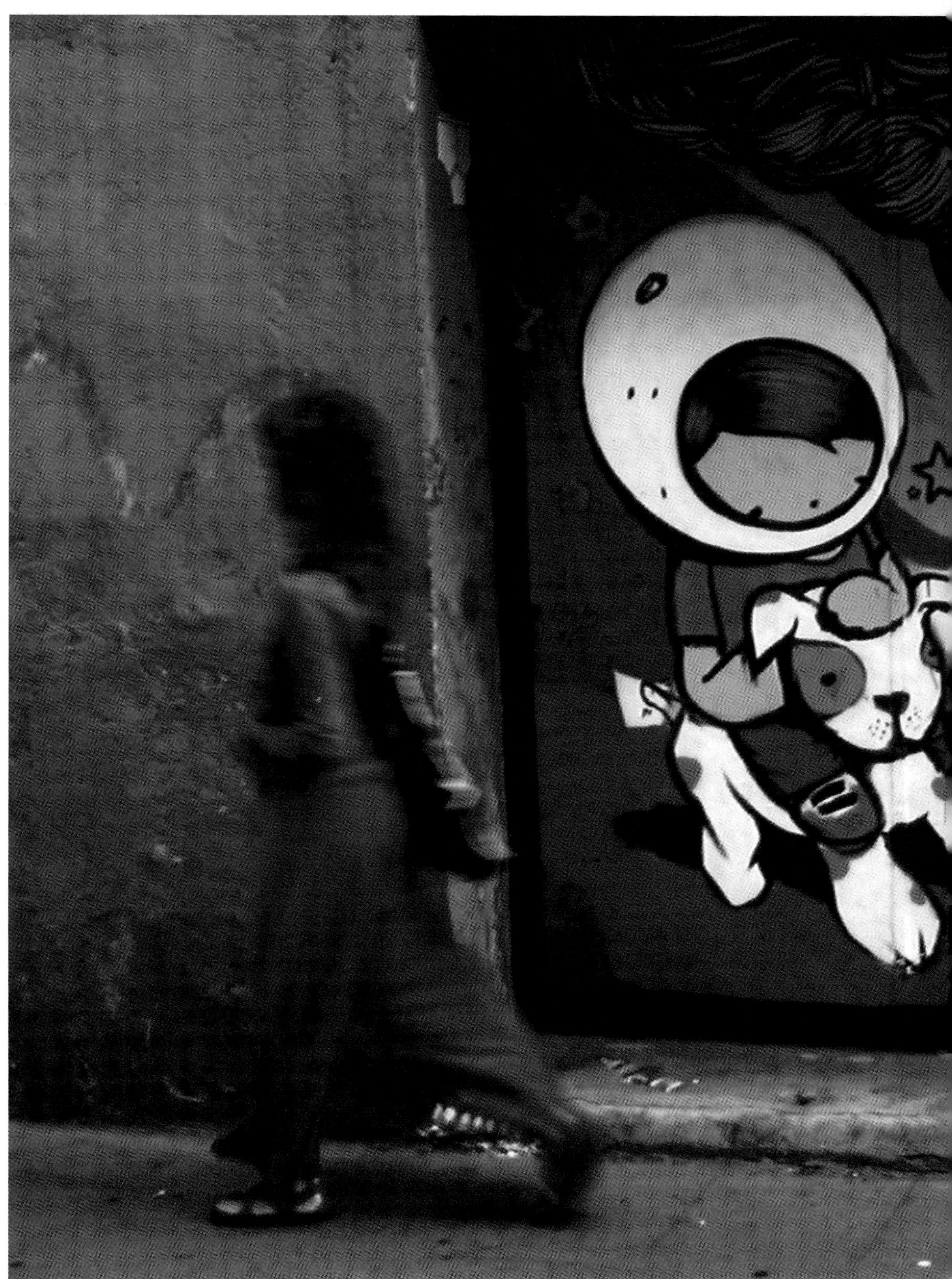

Rojo door with Lolo - Barcelona - 2006

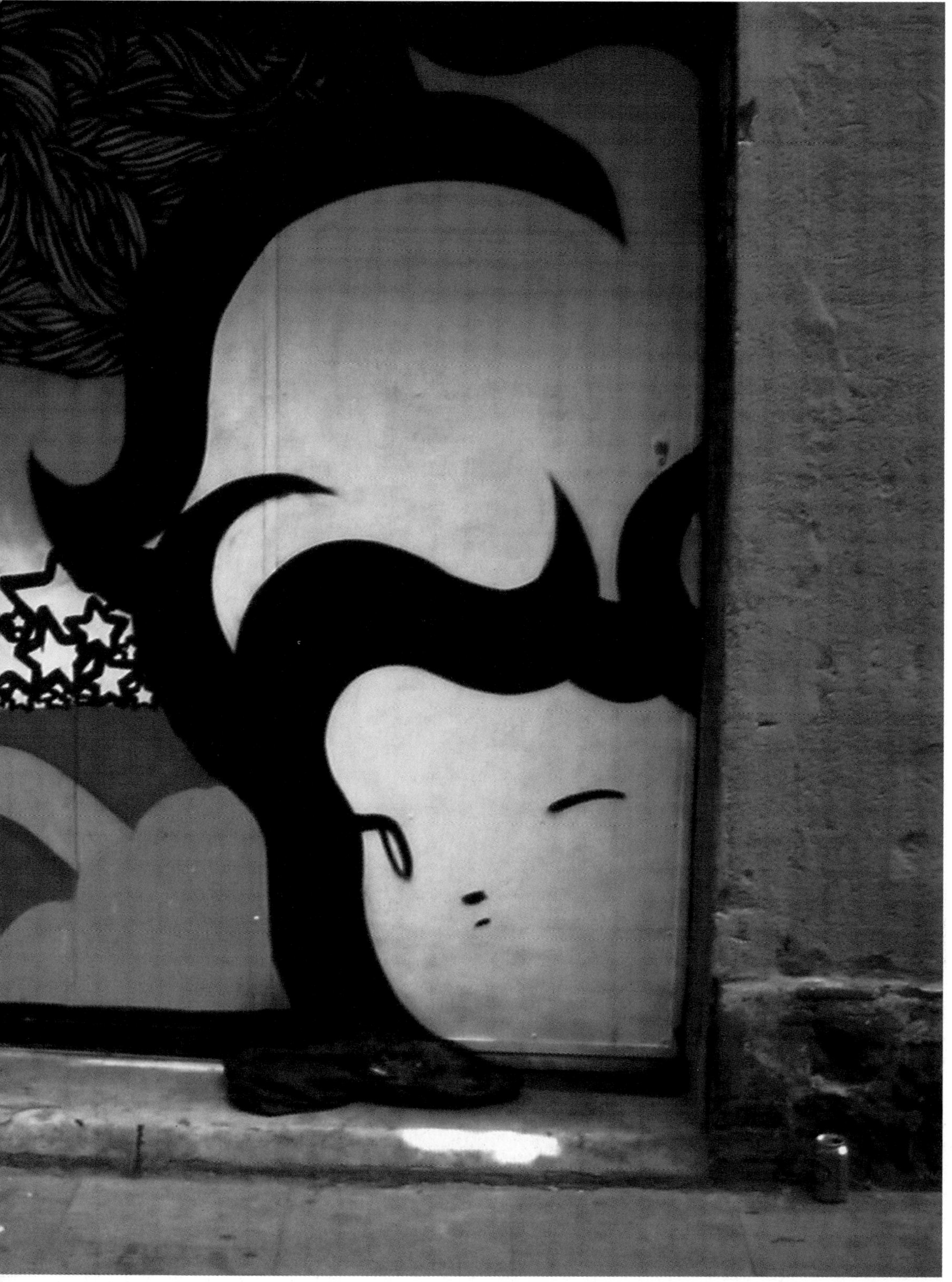

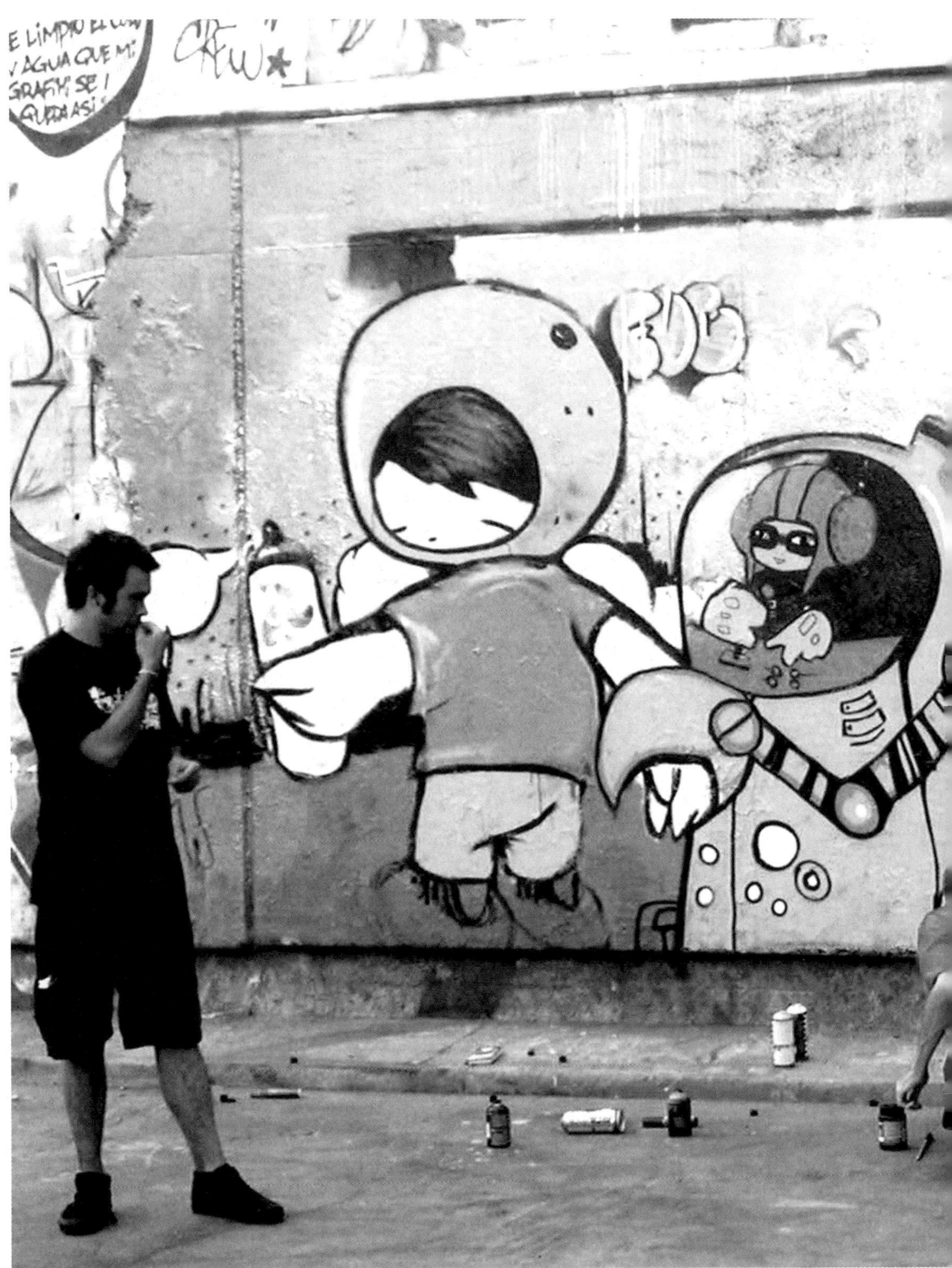

Graffiti with B-Toy - Barcelona - 2006

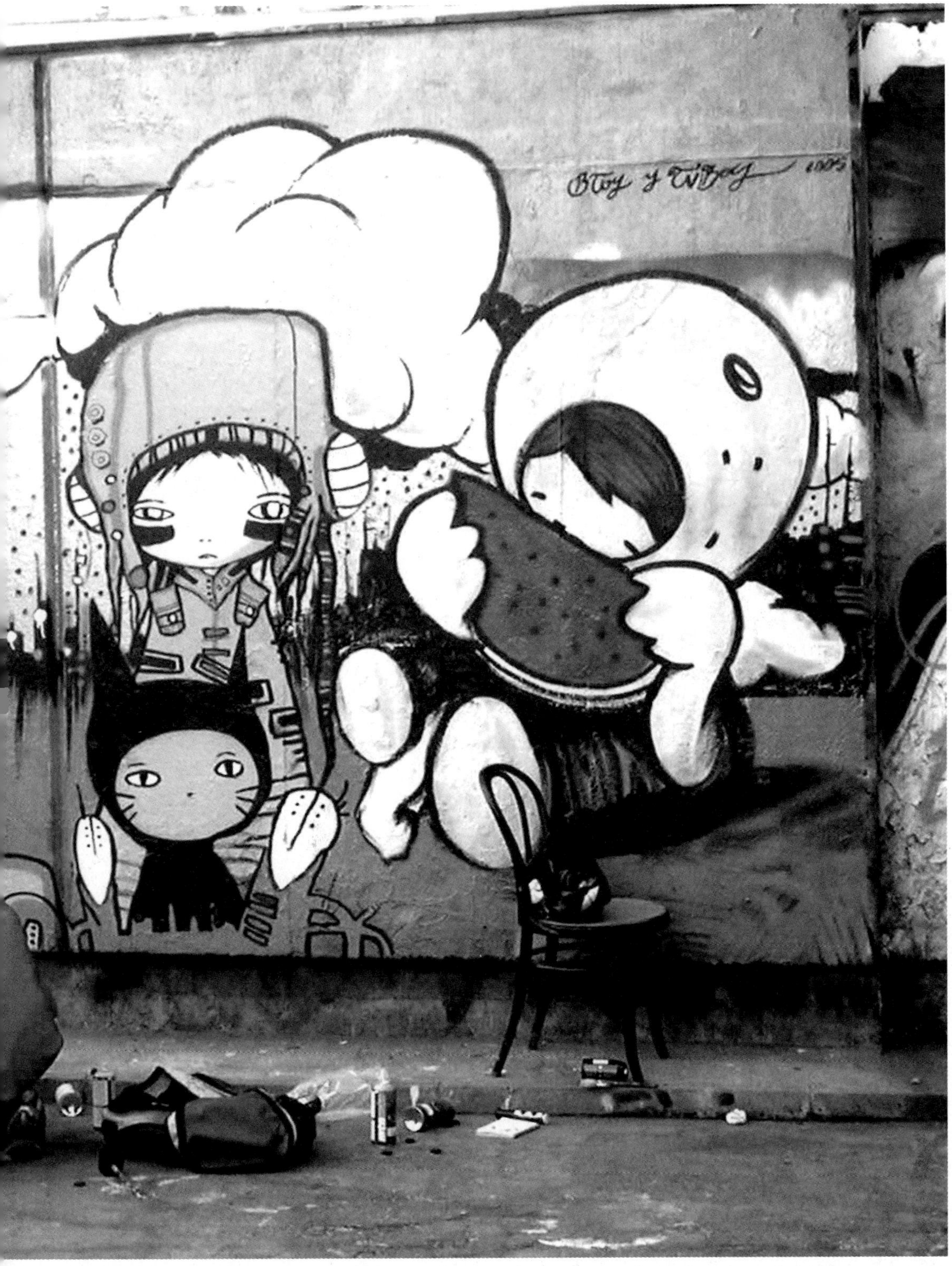

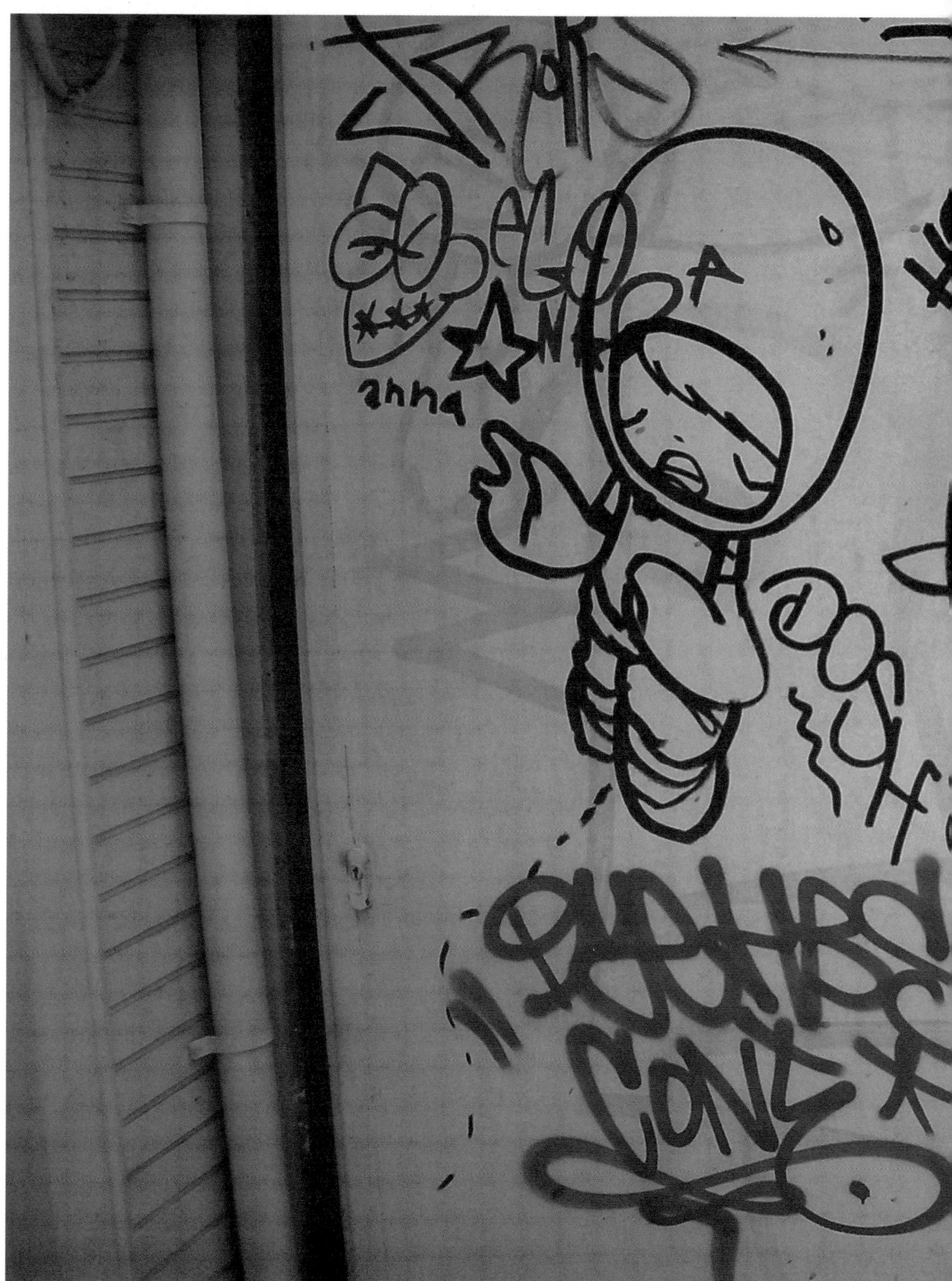

Tags - Barcelona - 2006

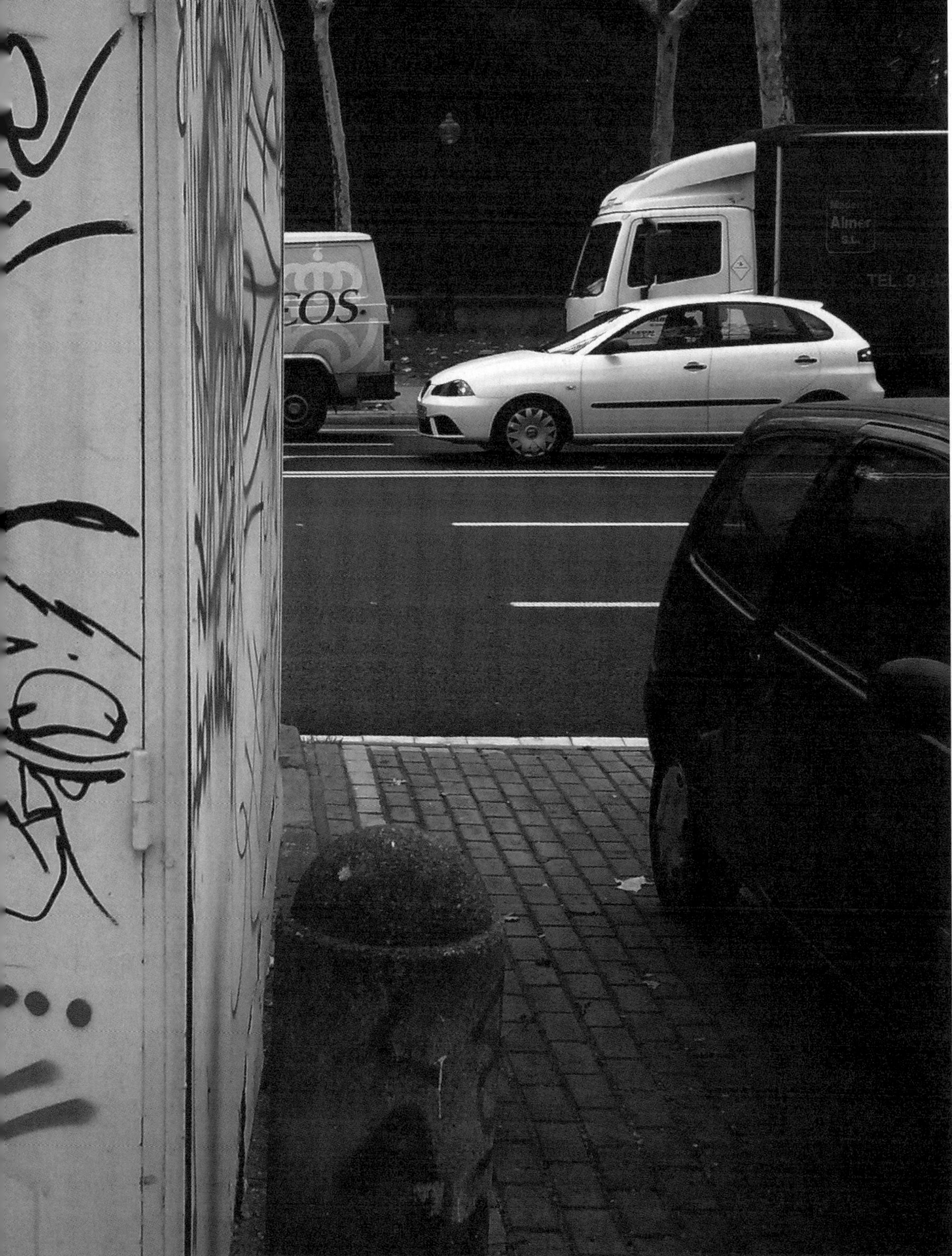

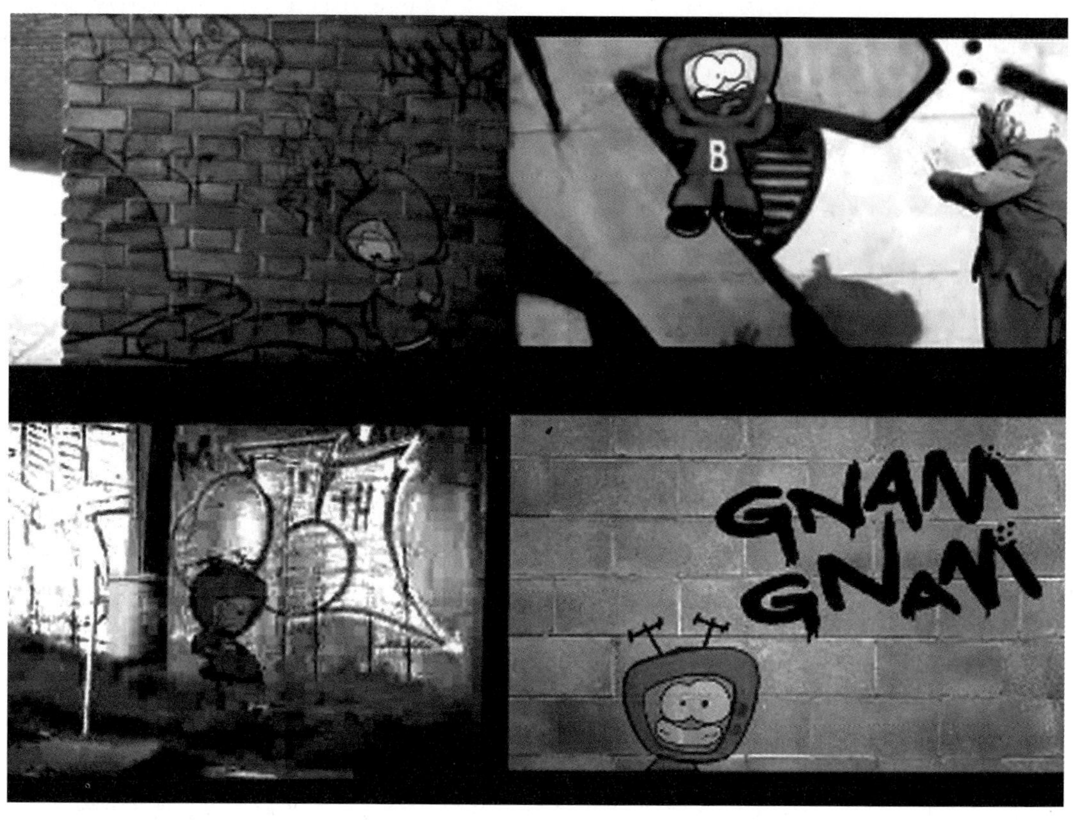

Not Tvboy!!! - Medias & big corporations start taking heavy inspiration from my work.... 2006

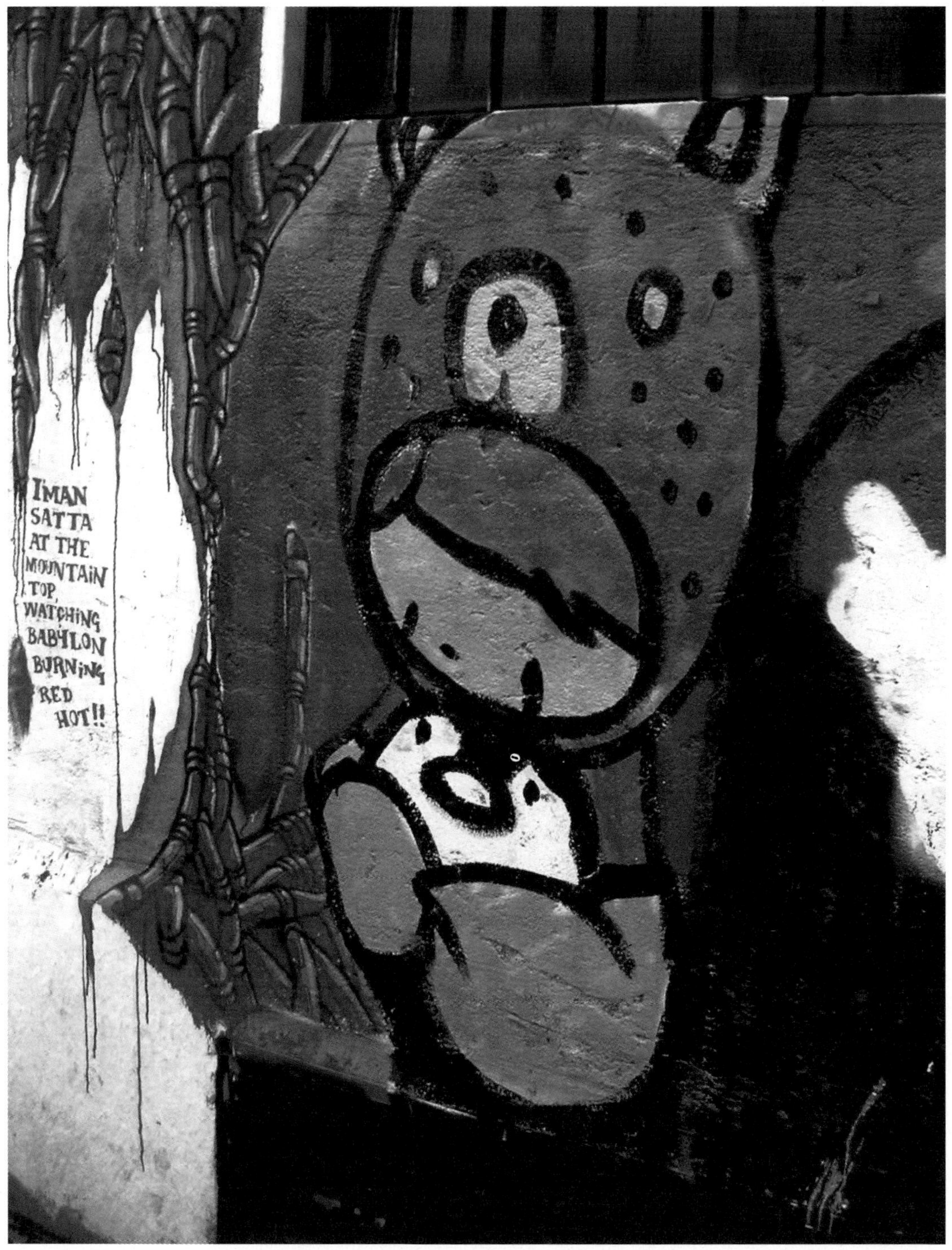

Urban intervention - Milan - 2005

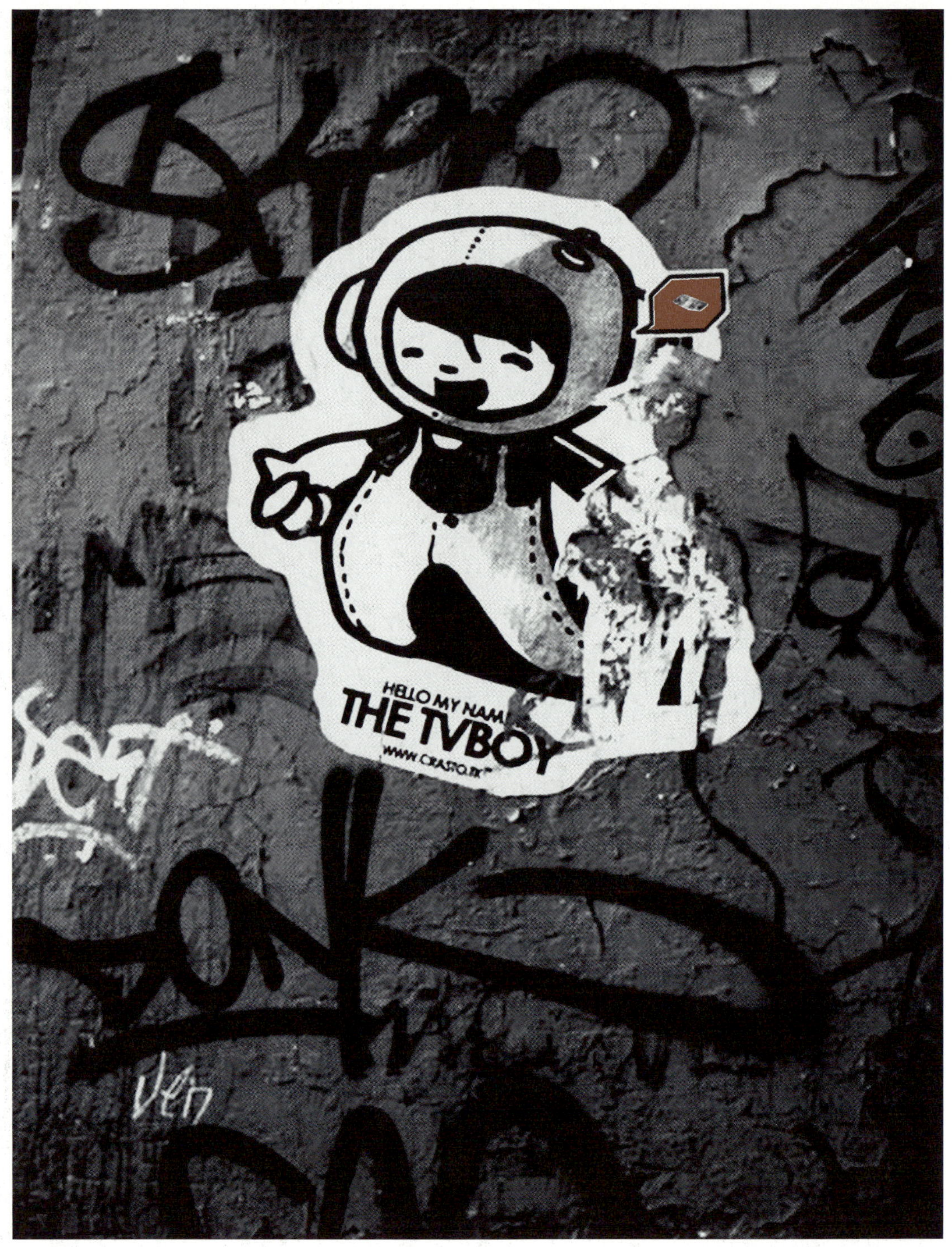

Urban intervention - Barcelona - 2005

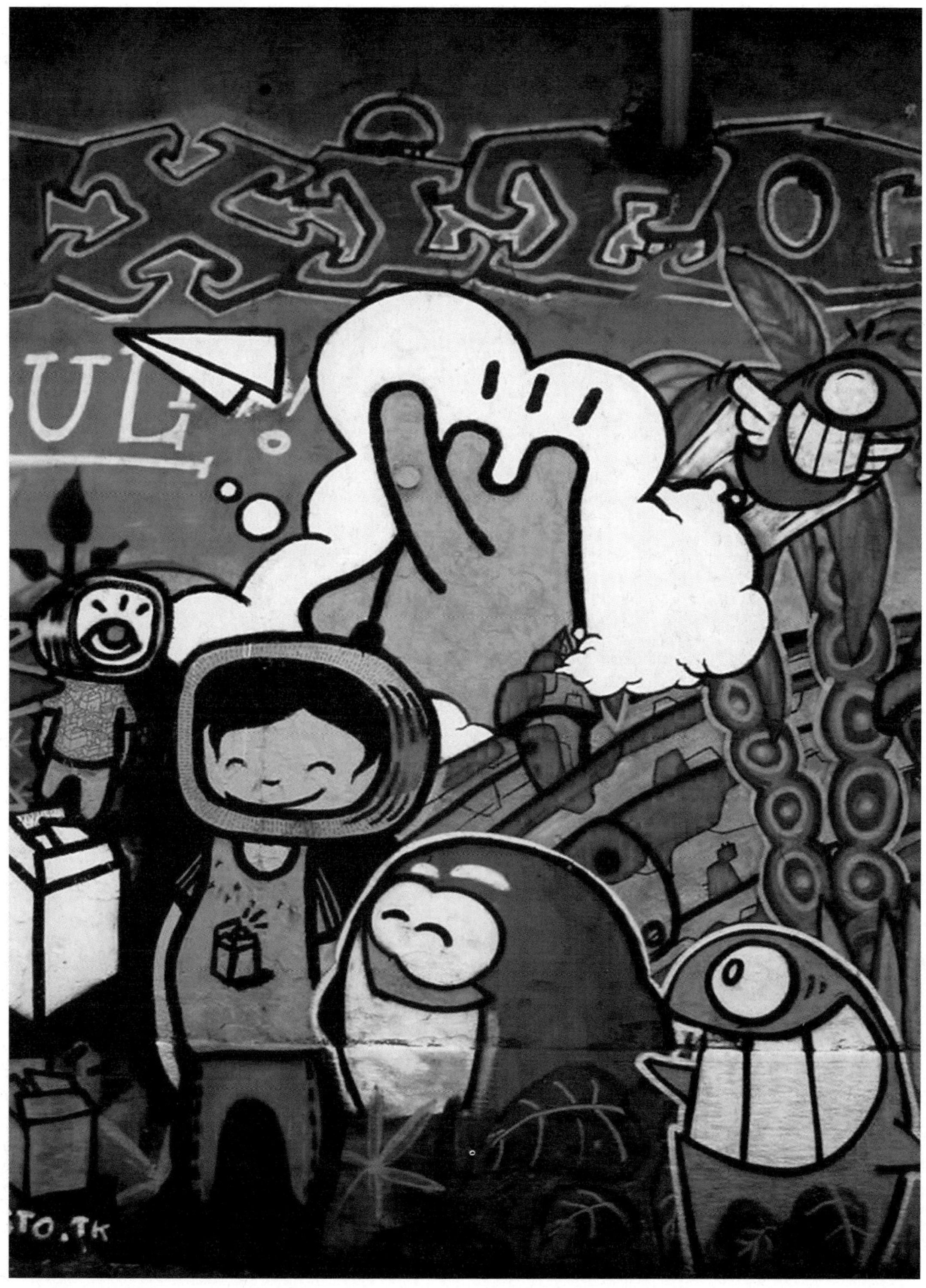

Urban intervention - Milan - 2004

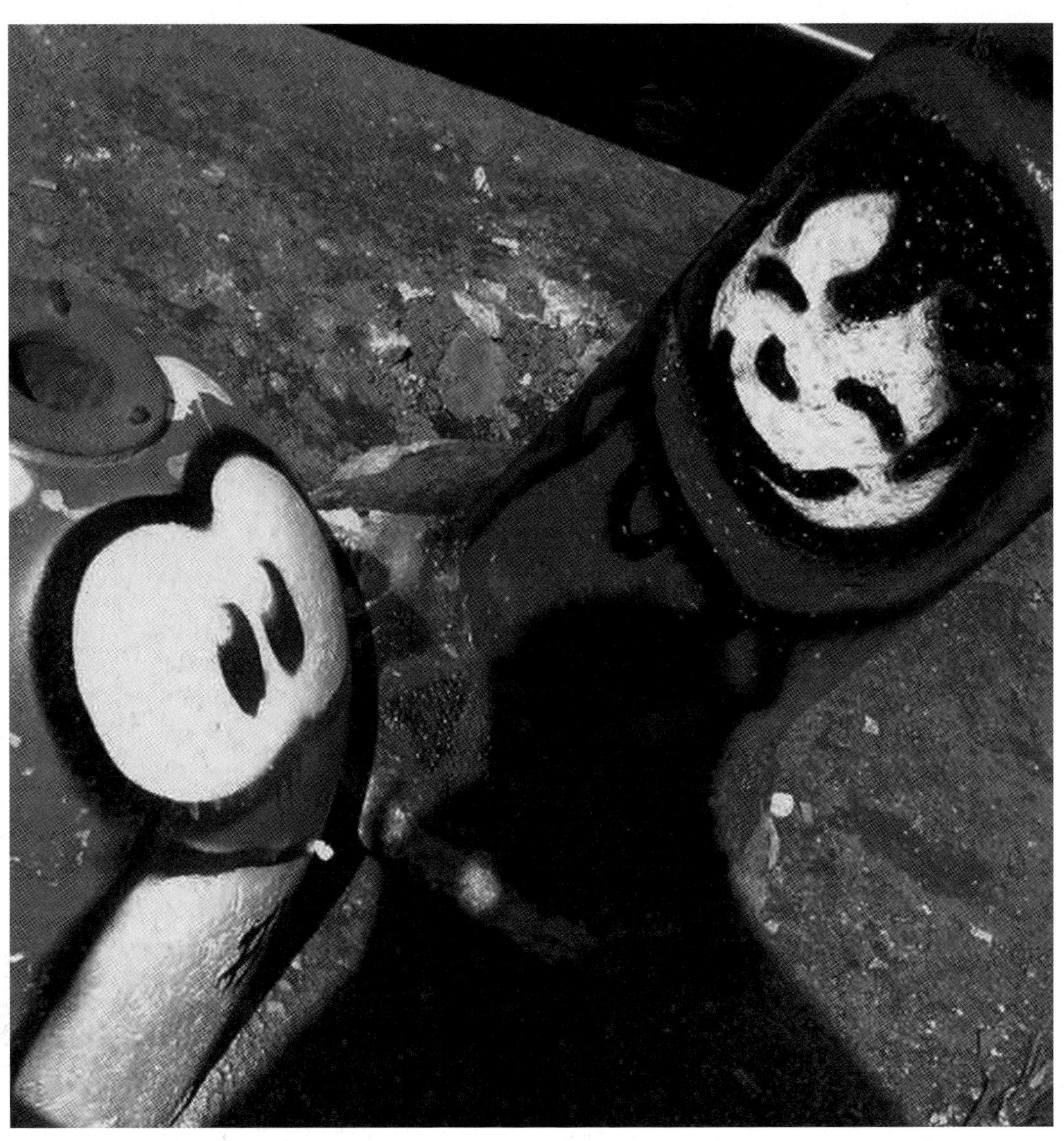

Urban intervention with Pao - Milan - 2004

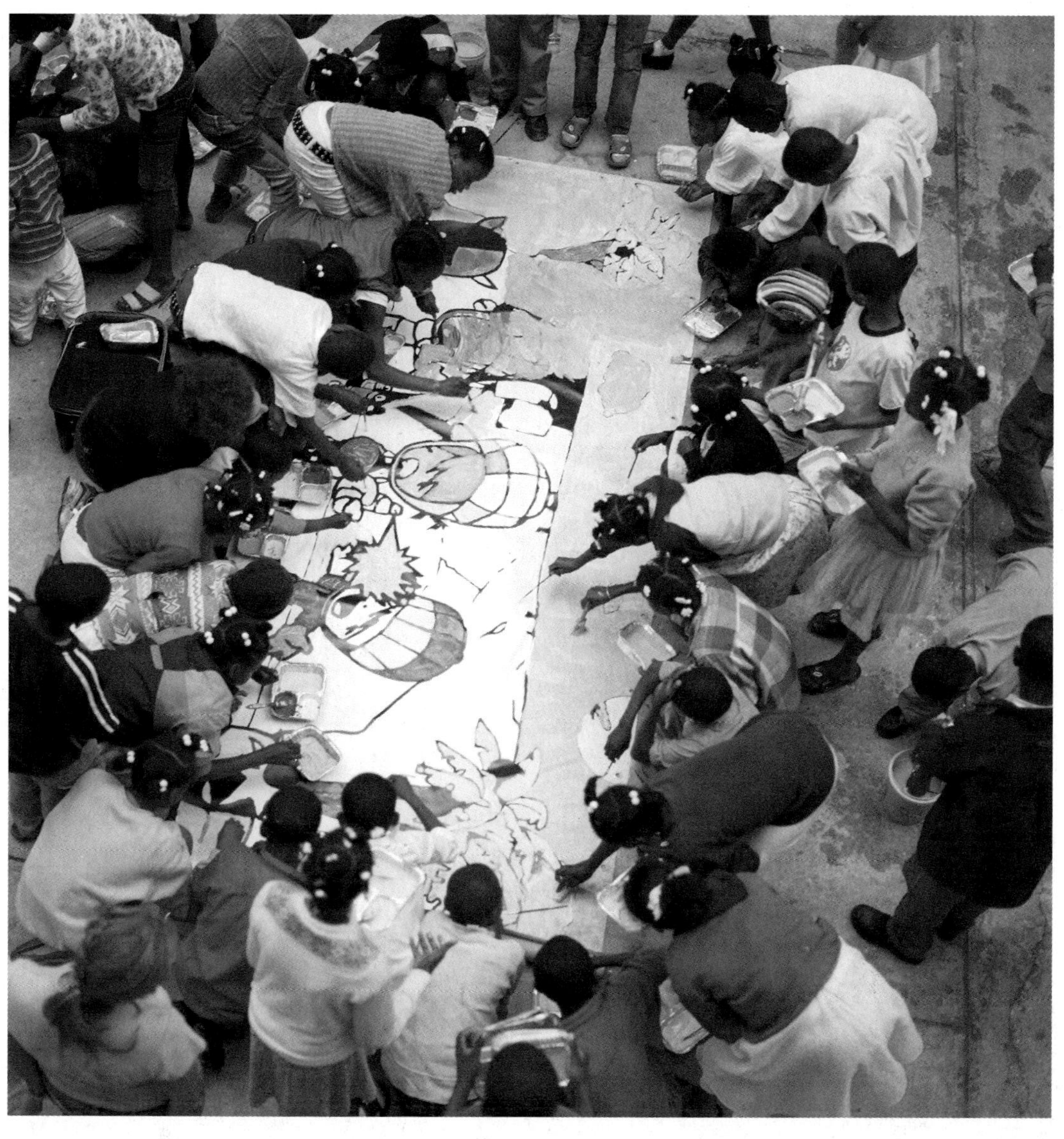

Port Au Prince, HAITI - Charity project with Art Kitchen, Nescafé, N.P.H. Fondazione Rava - 2007

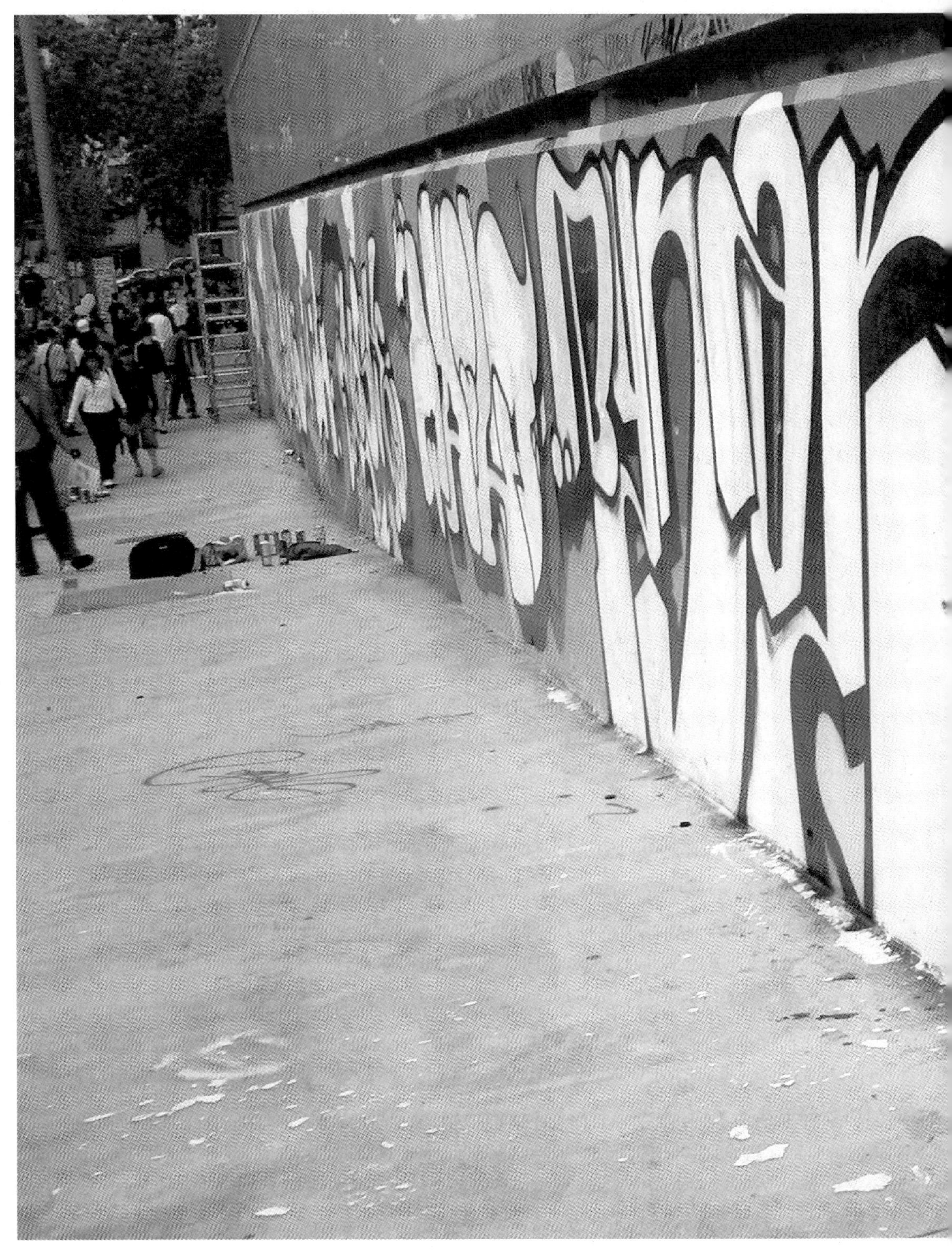

Urban intervention - Urbanfunke Festival - Barcelona - 2006

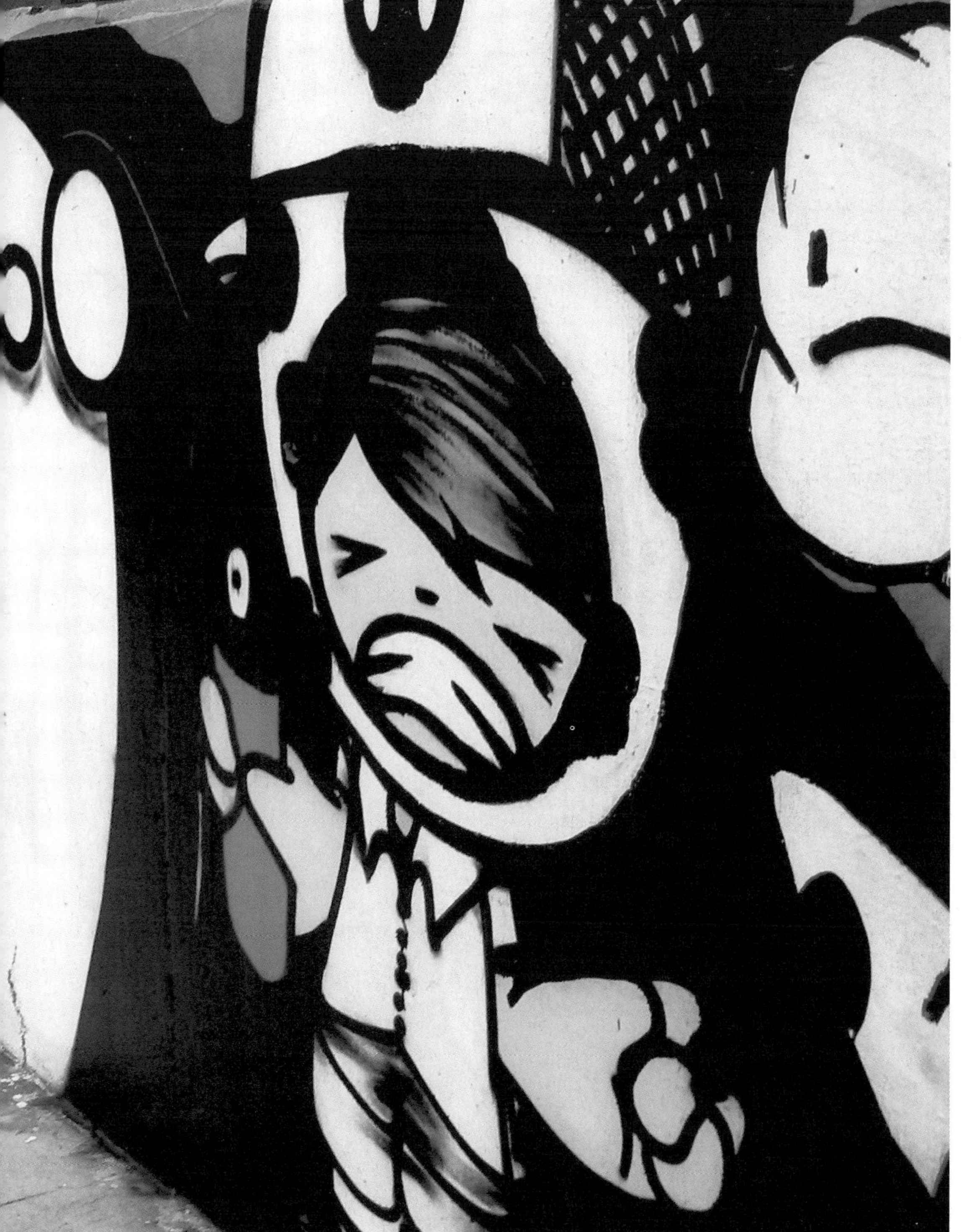

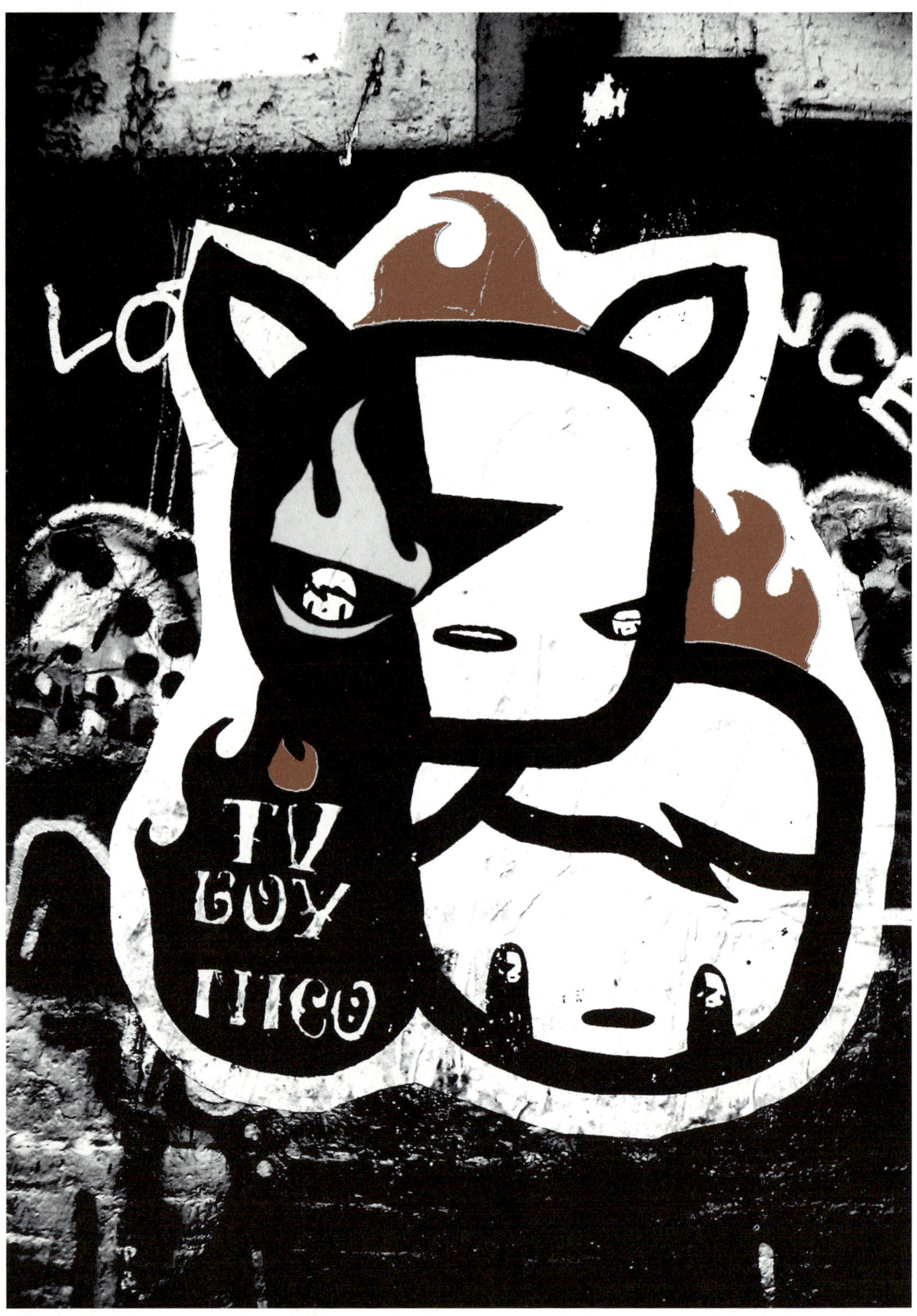

Urban intervention - Barcelona - 2006

STUFF

Start a Revolution without Weapons

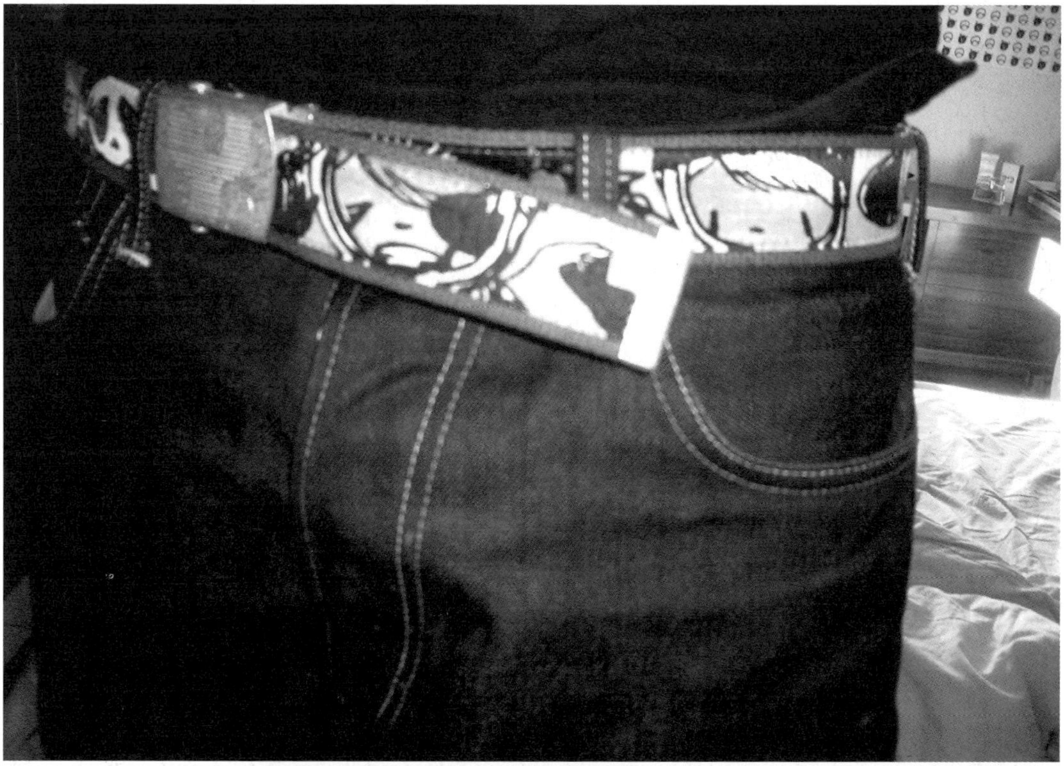

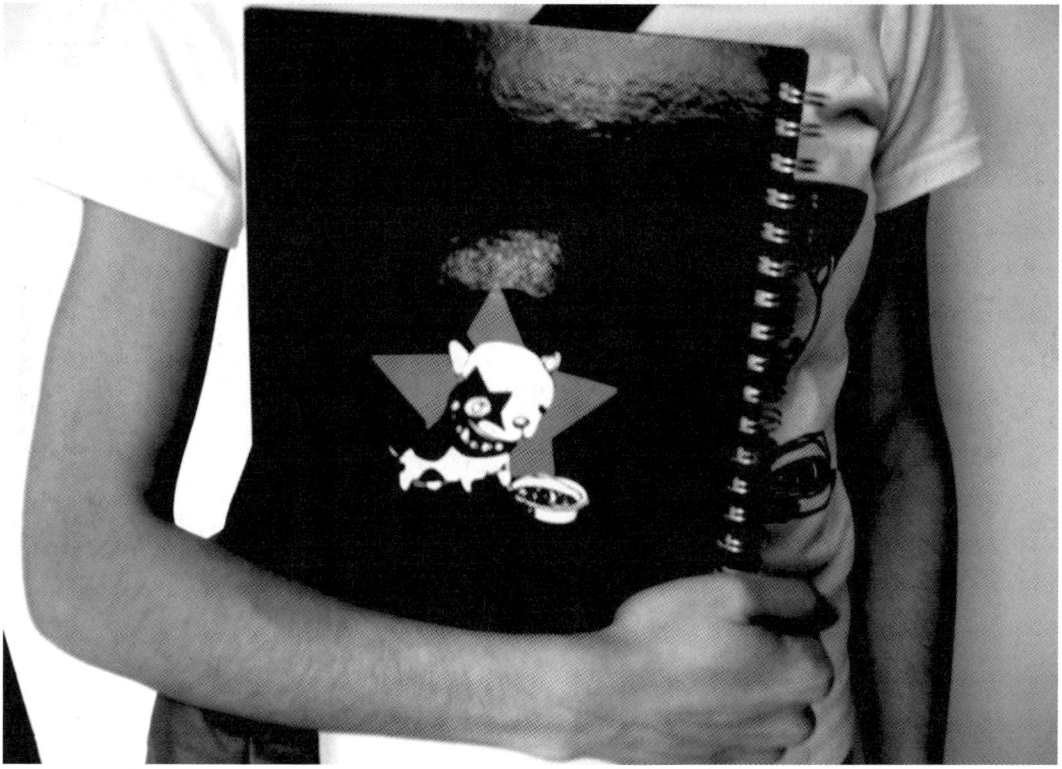

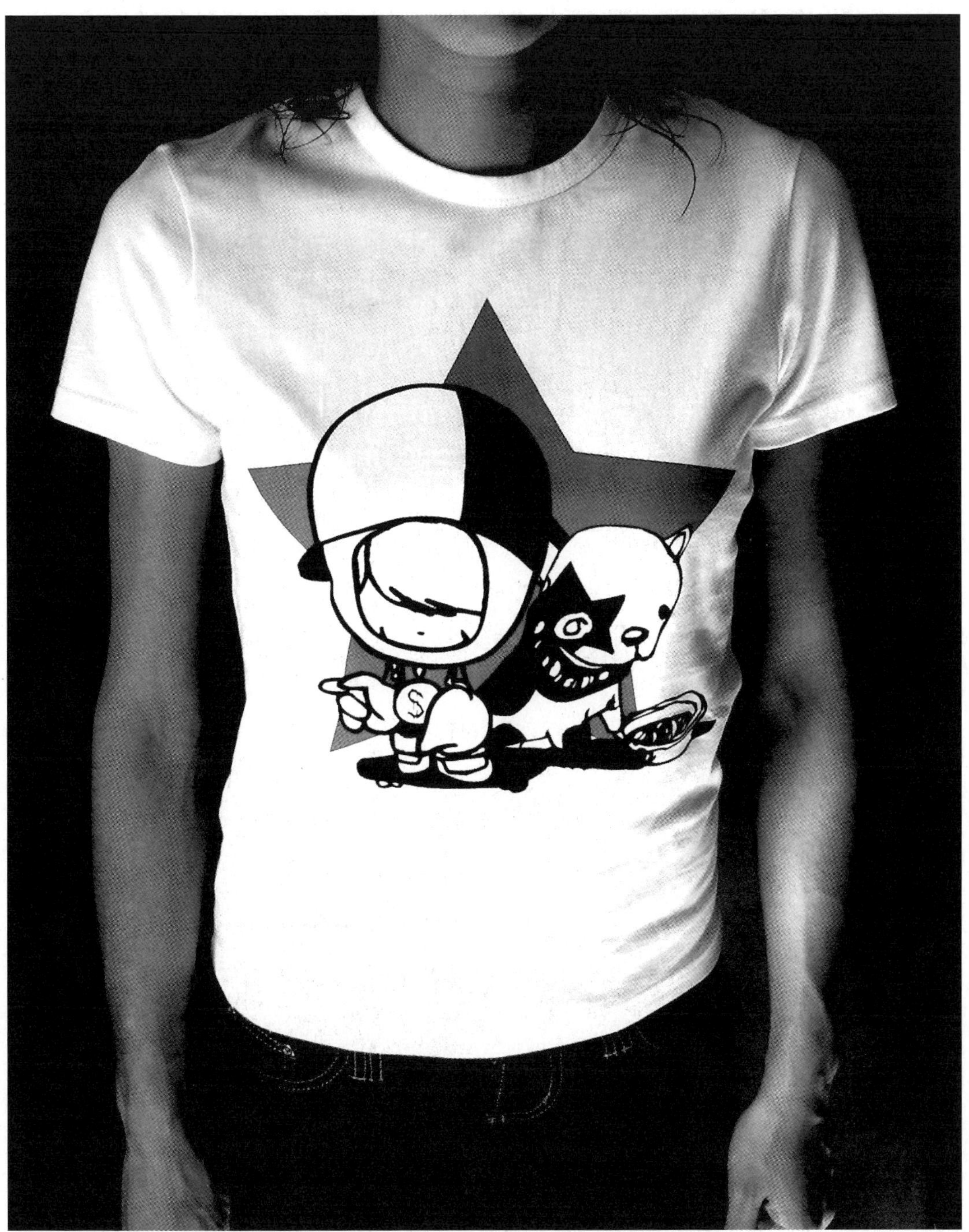

Wearing Tvboy - belt, stationery, tees

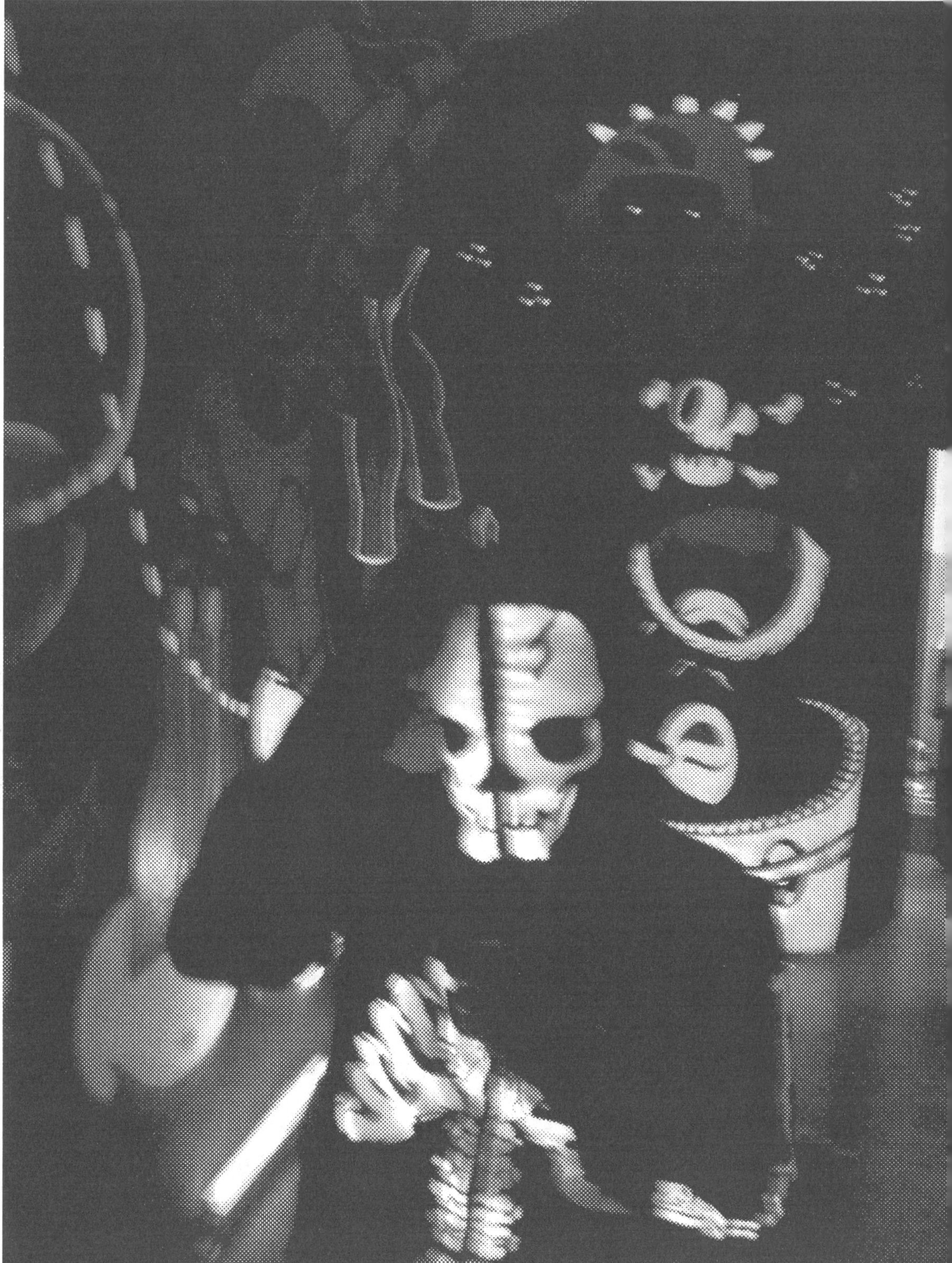

INSTALLATIONS

Start a Revolution without Weapons

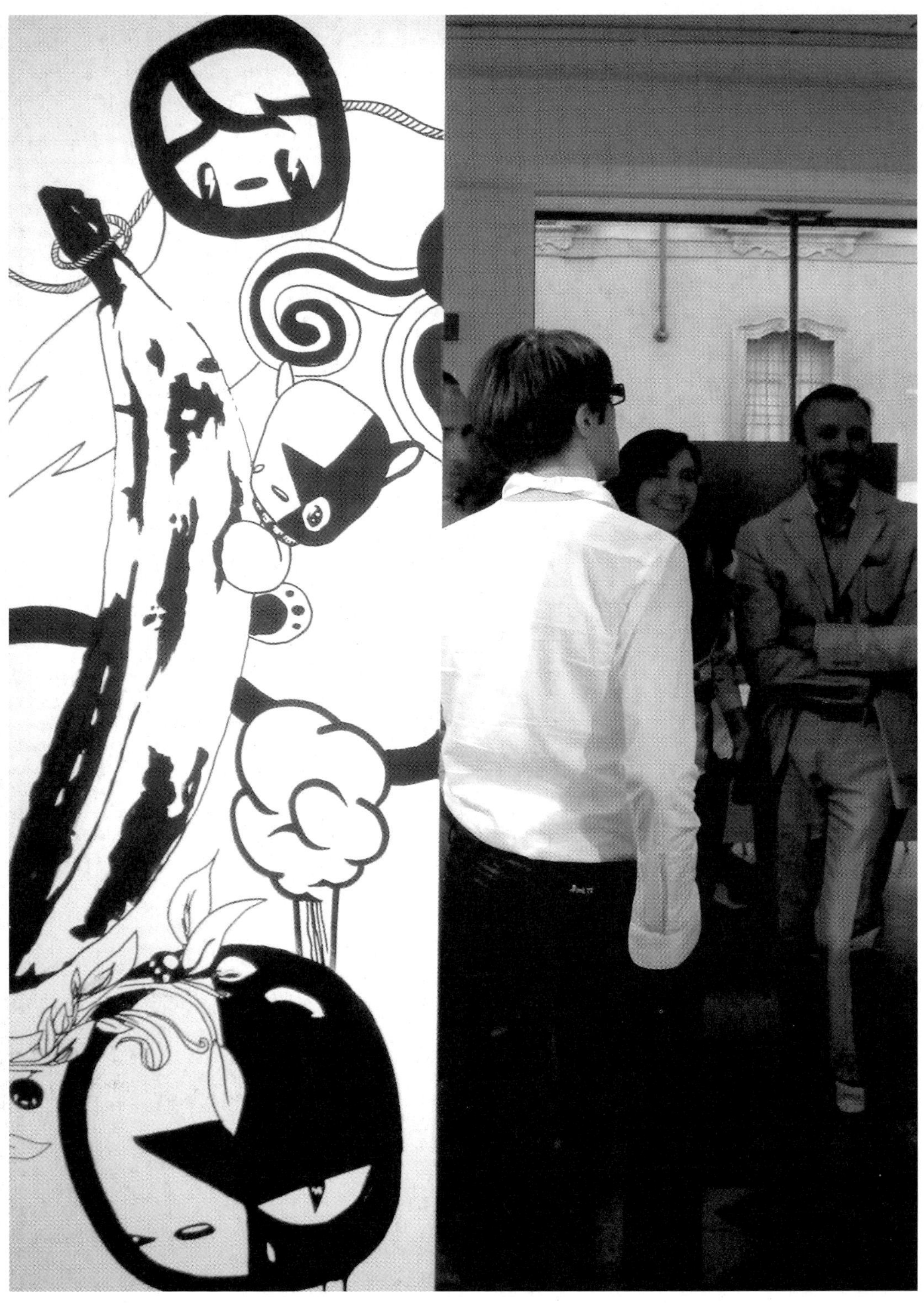

Installation at Byblos Art Gallery - Verona - 2007

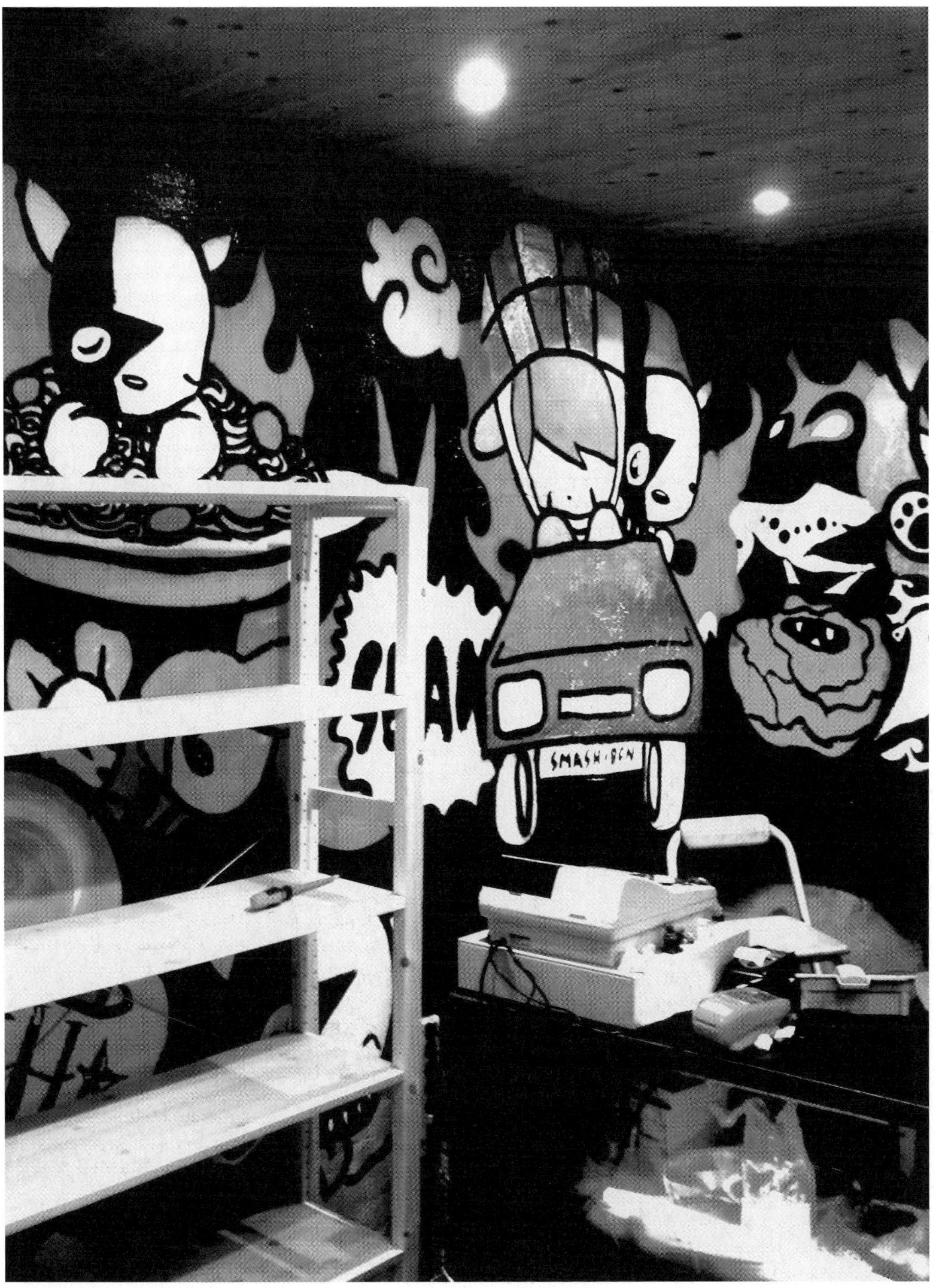

Smash Shop - Barcelona - 2006

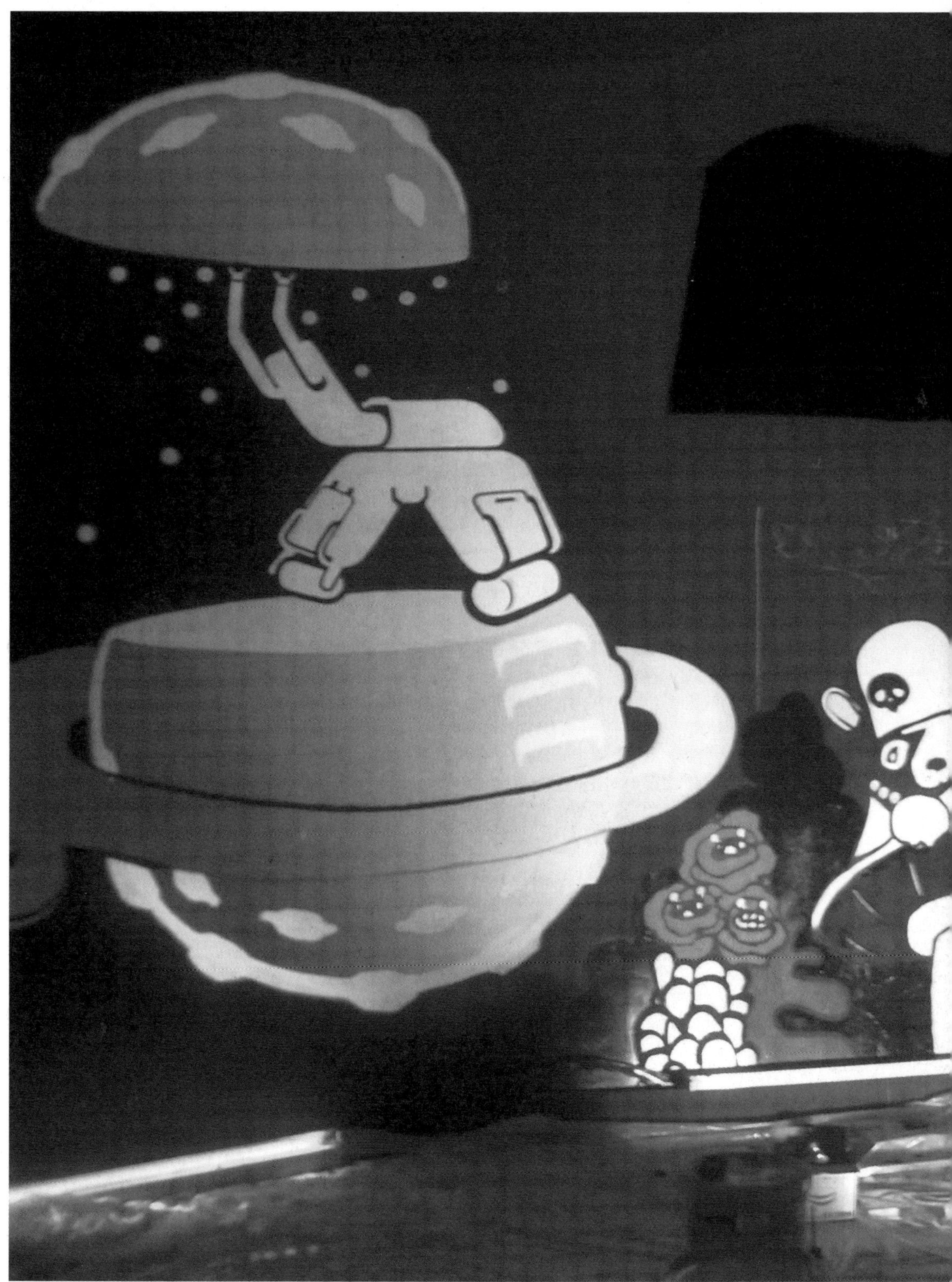

Monztaah! Installation - (with Sat One, Besdo Garcia) Zaragoza, Museo de Historia - 2006

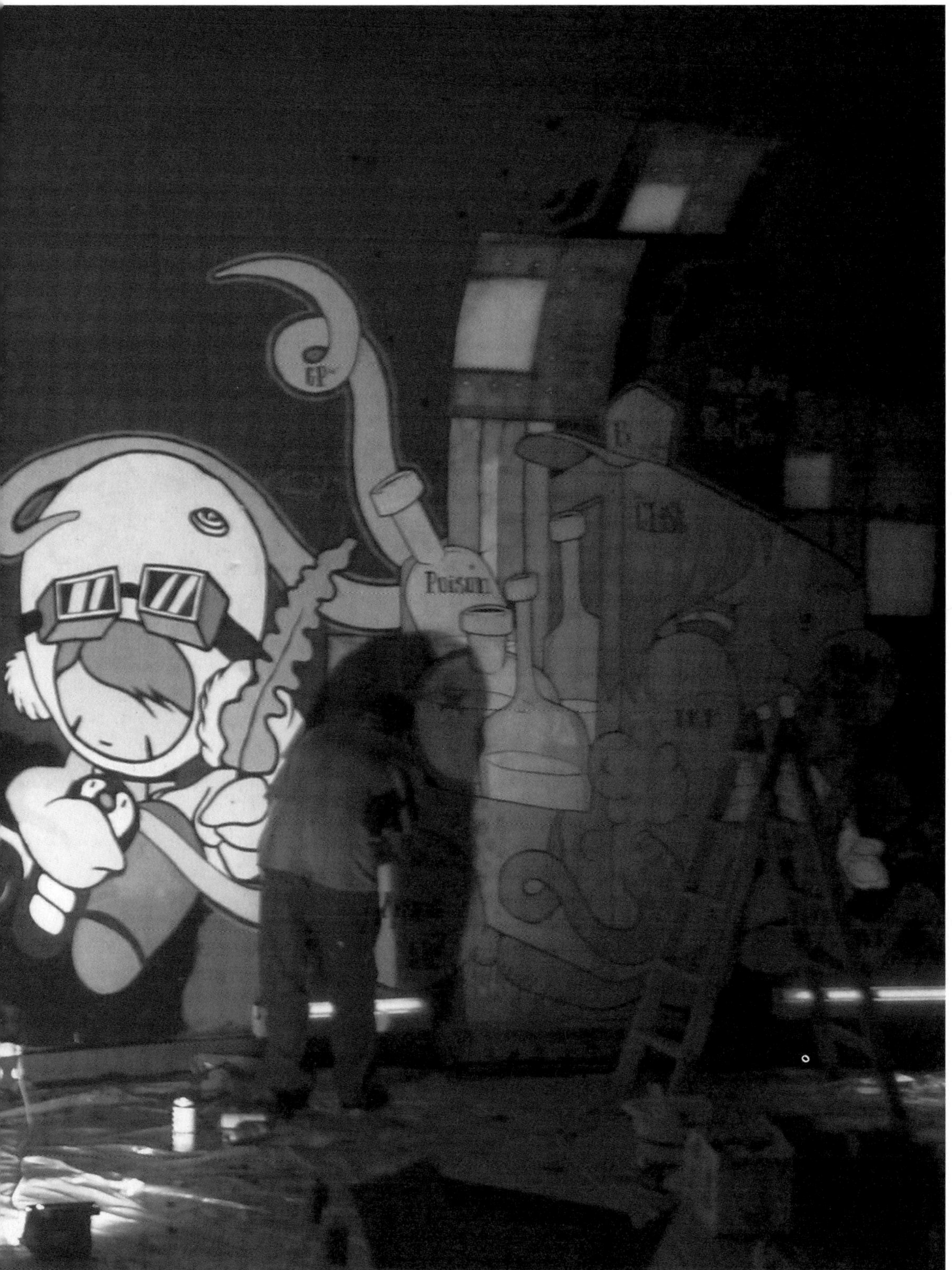

GP
Poison

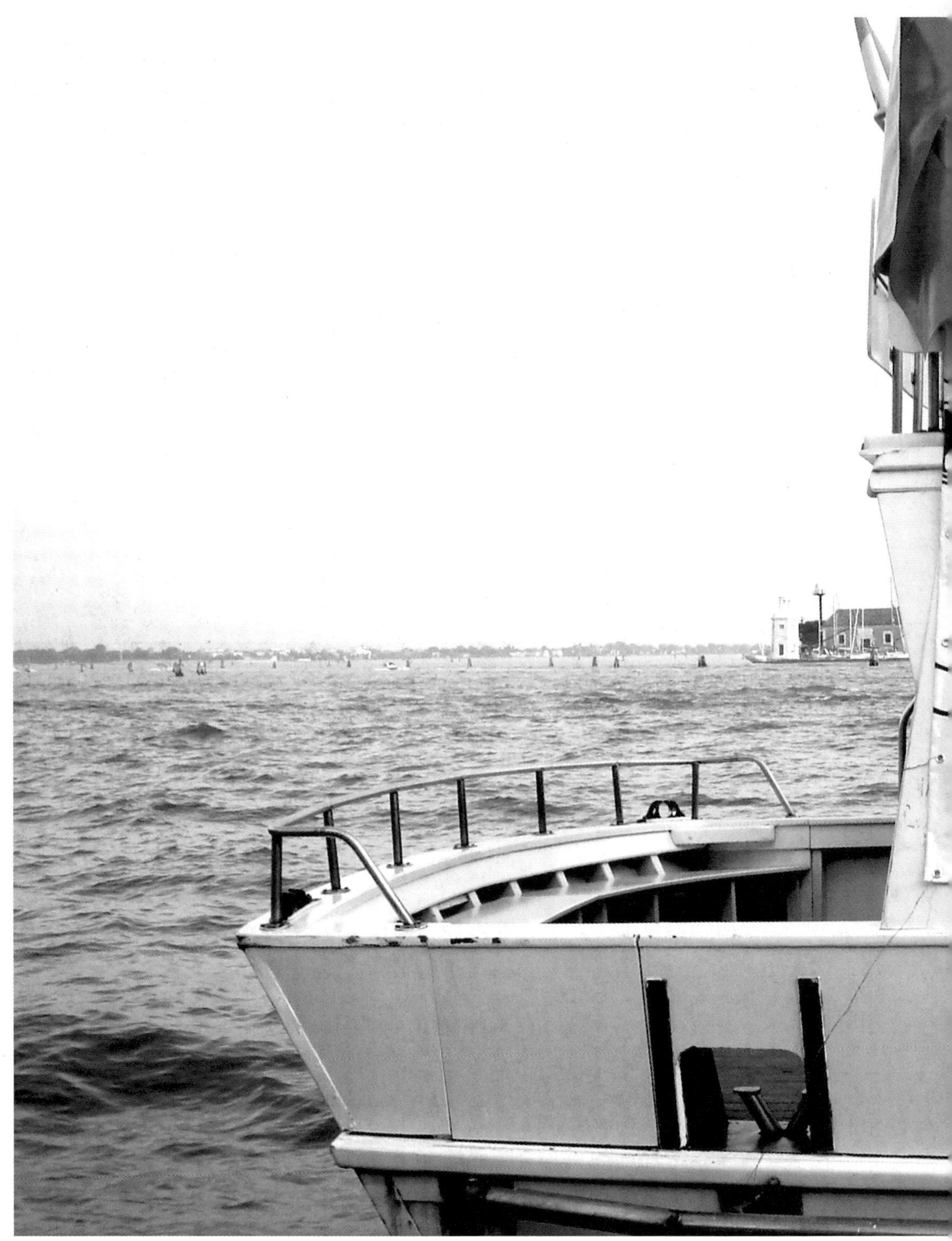

Tvboy Boat - Venice - 2007

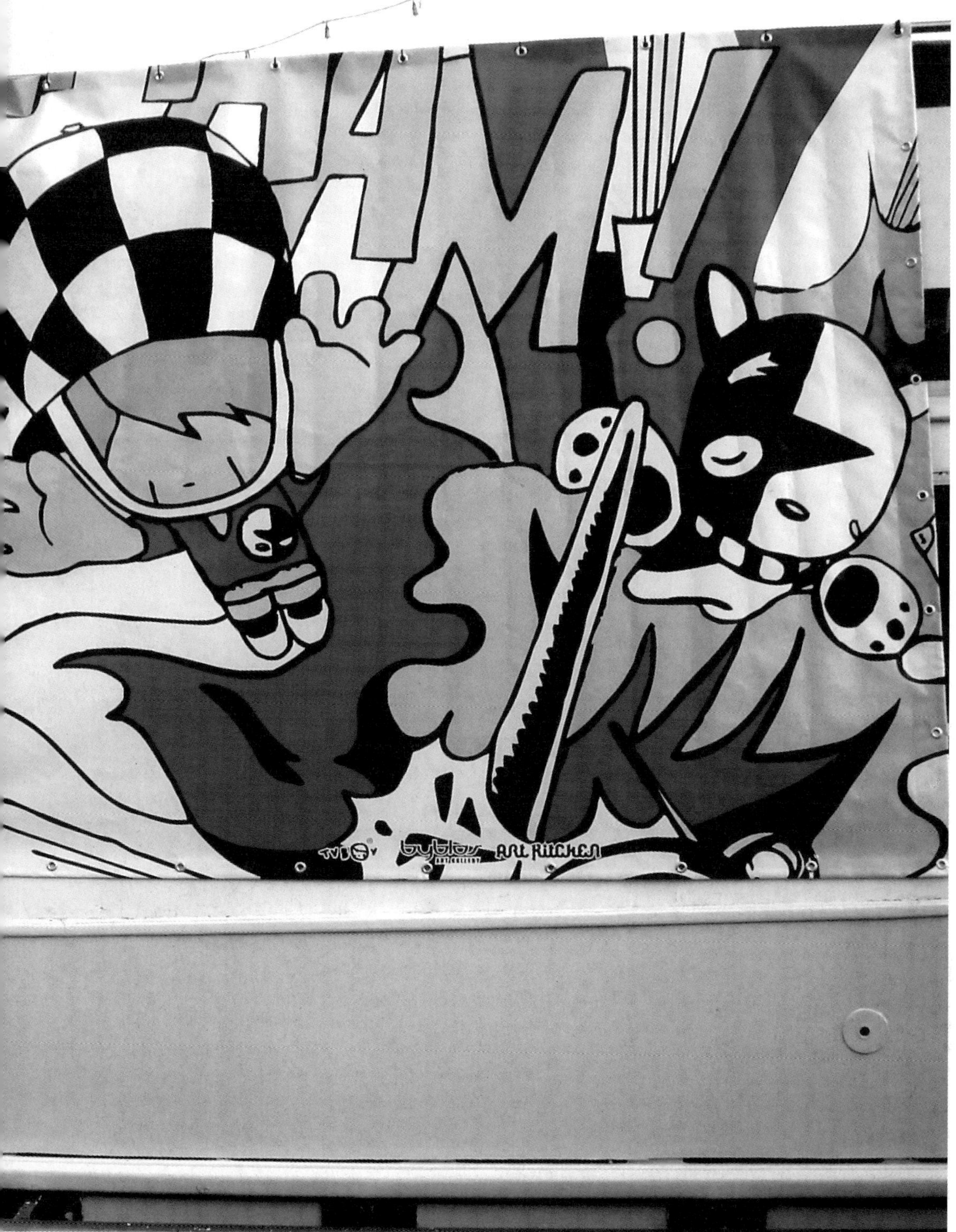

TVBOY
byblos ART GALLERY
ART KITCHEN

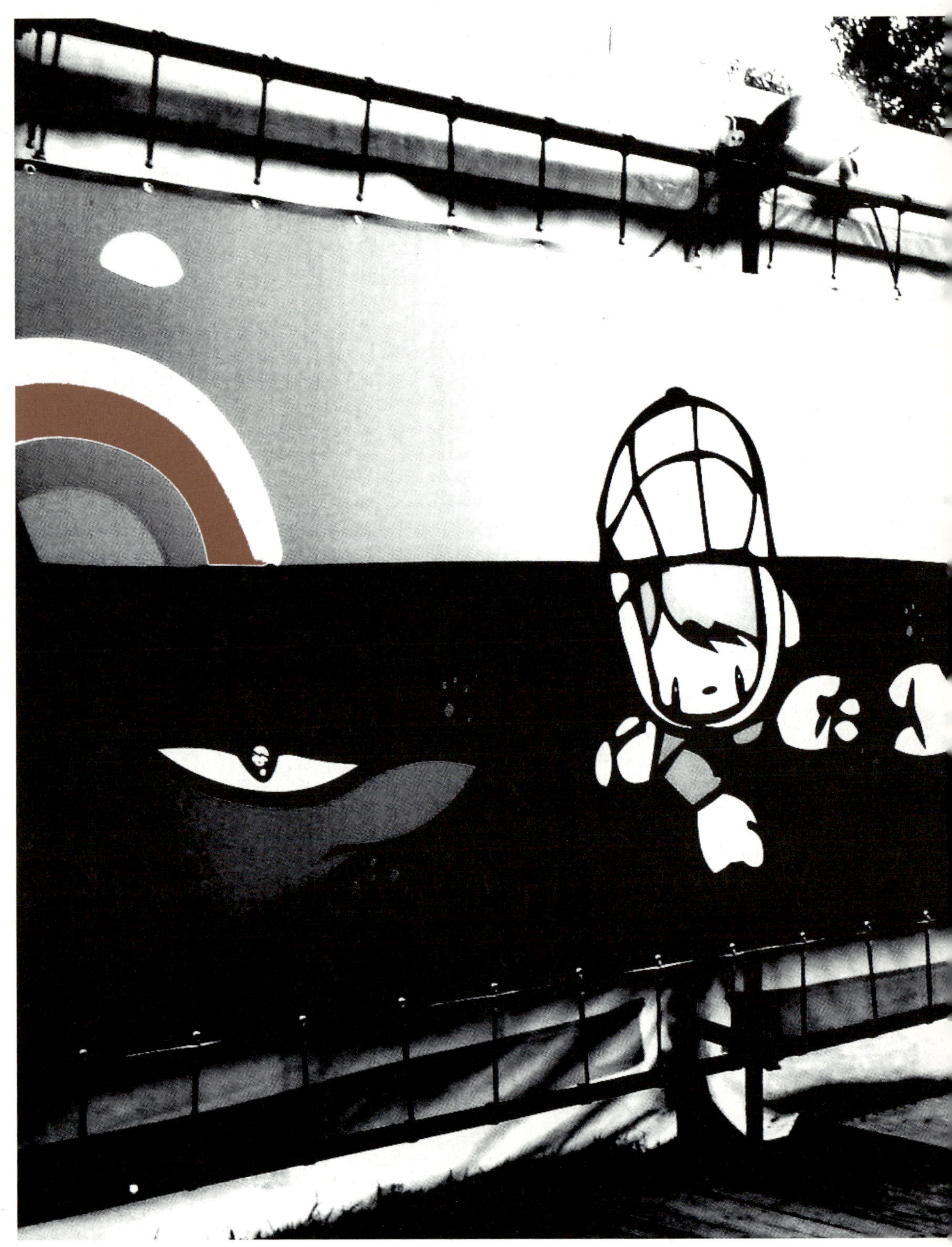

Unity is Strenght - Milano, Festa dell'Unità - 2007

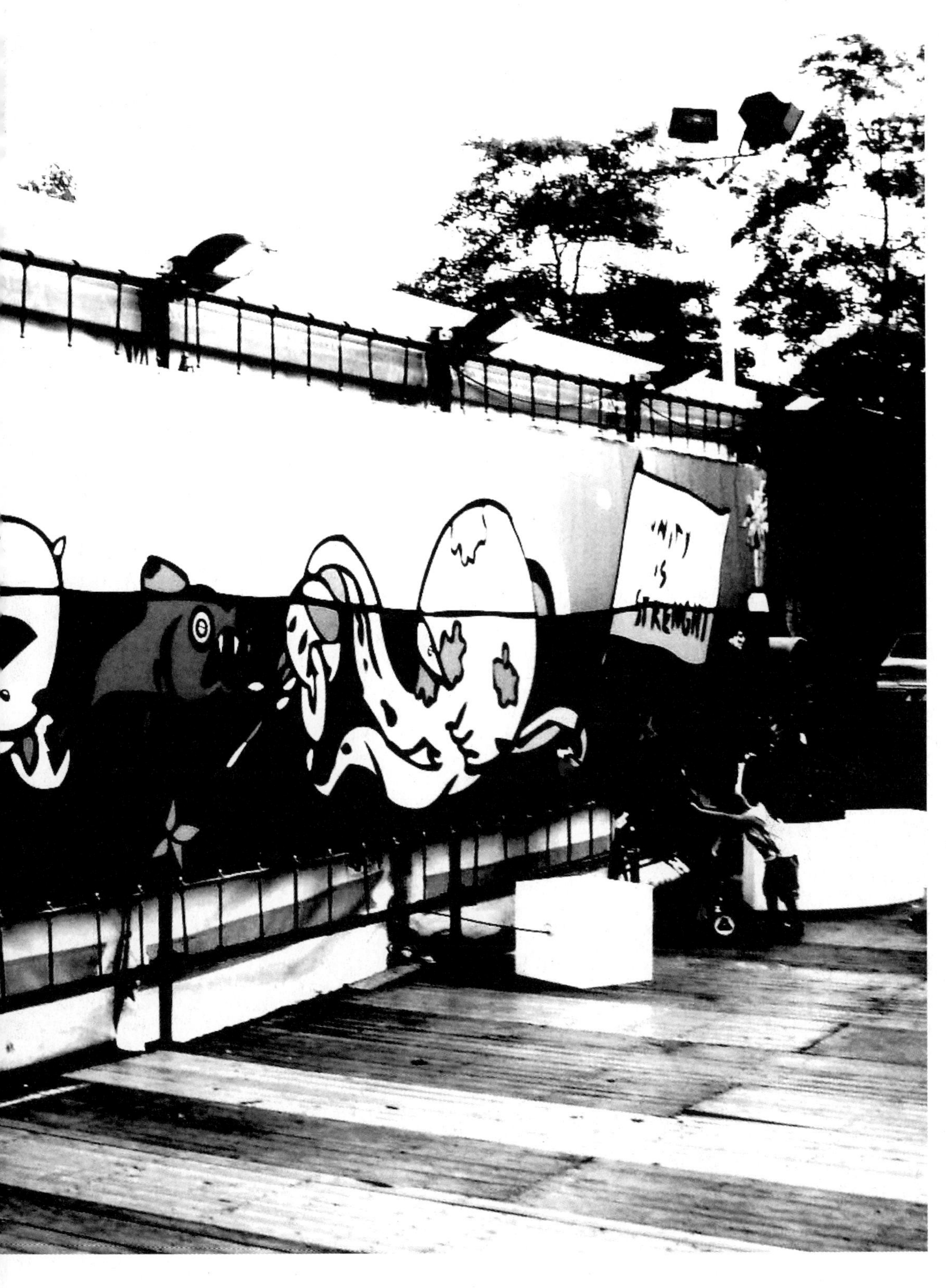
UNITY
IS
STRENGHT

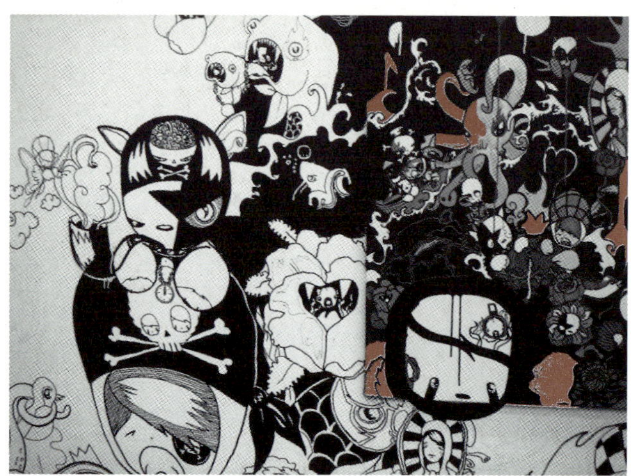

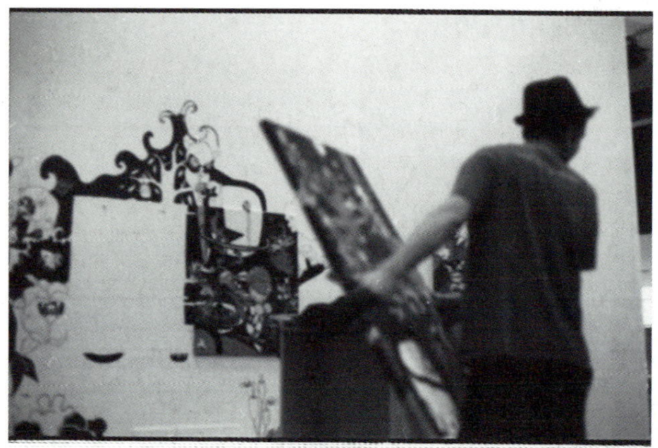

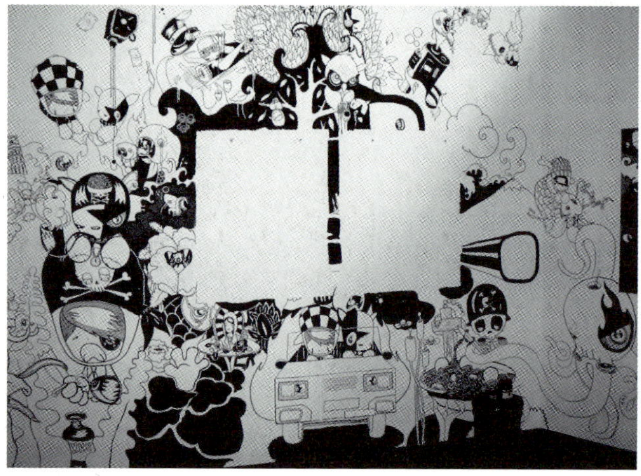

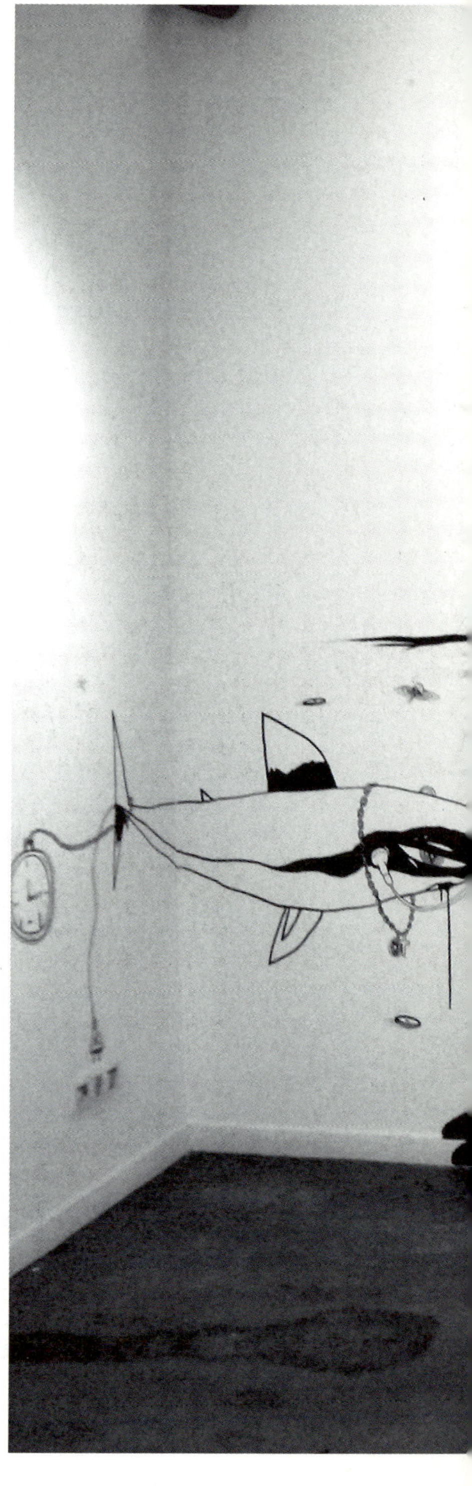

Missed canvases installation - "Street art sweet art" Padiglione d'Arte Contemporanea - Milan - 2007

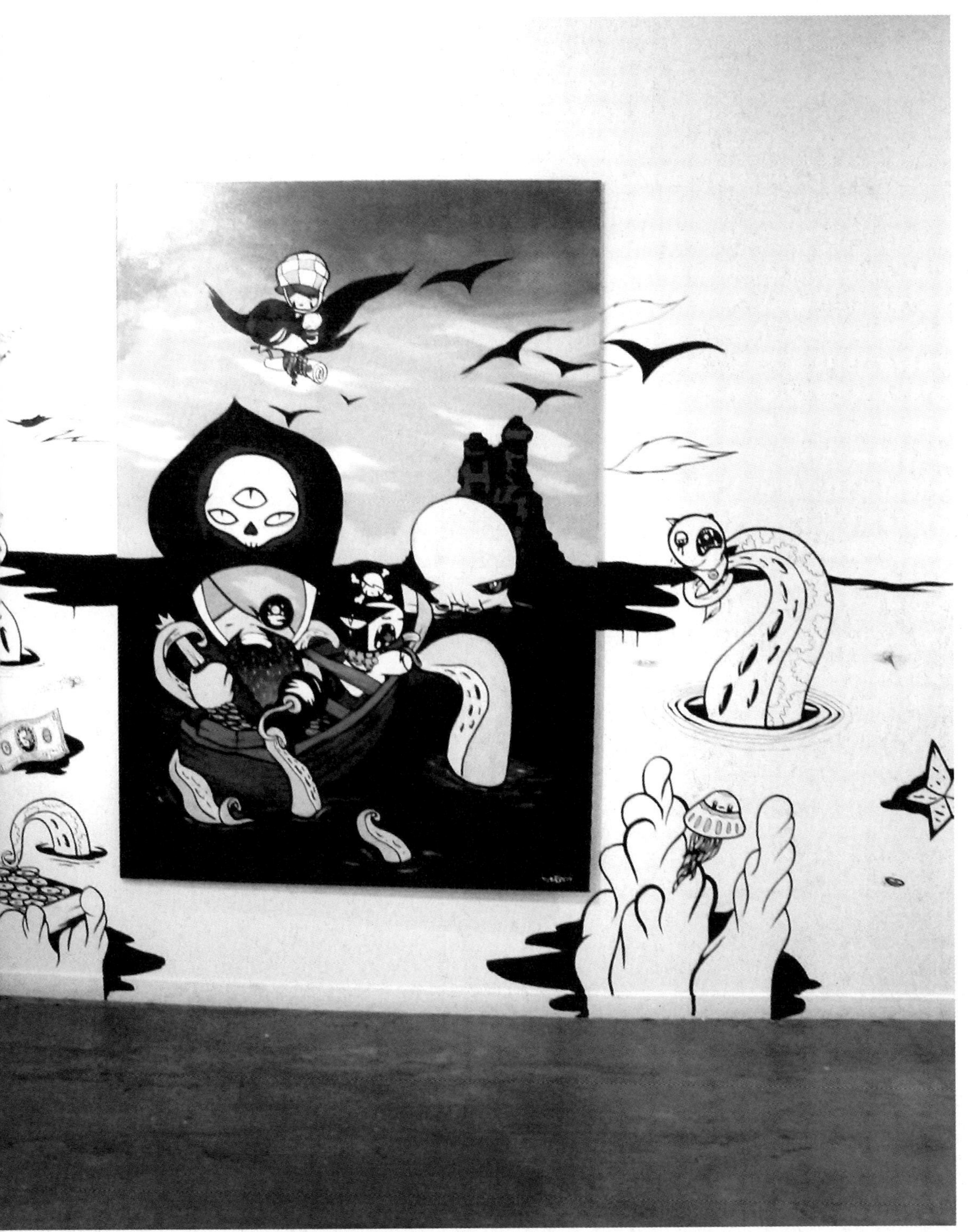

Sea Installation - "Please don't die" Personal exhibition at Iguapop Gallery - Barcelona - 2007

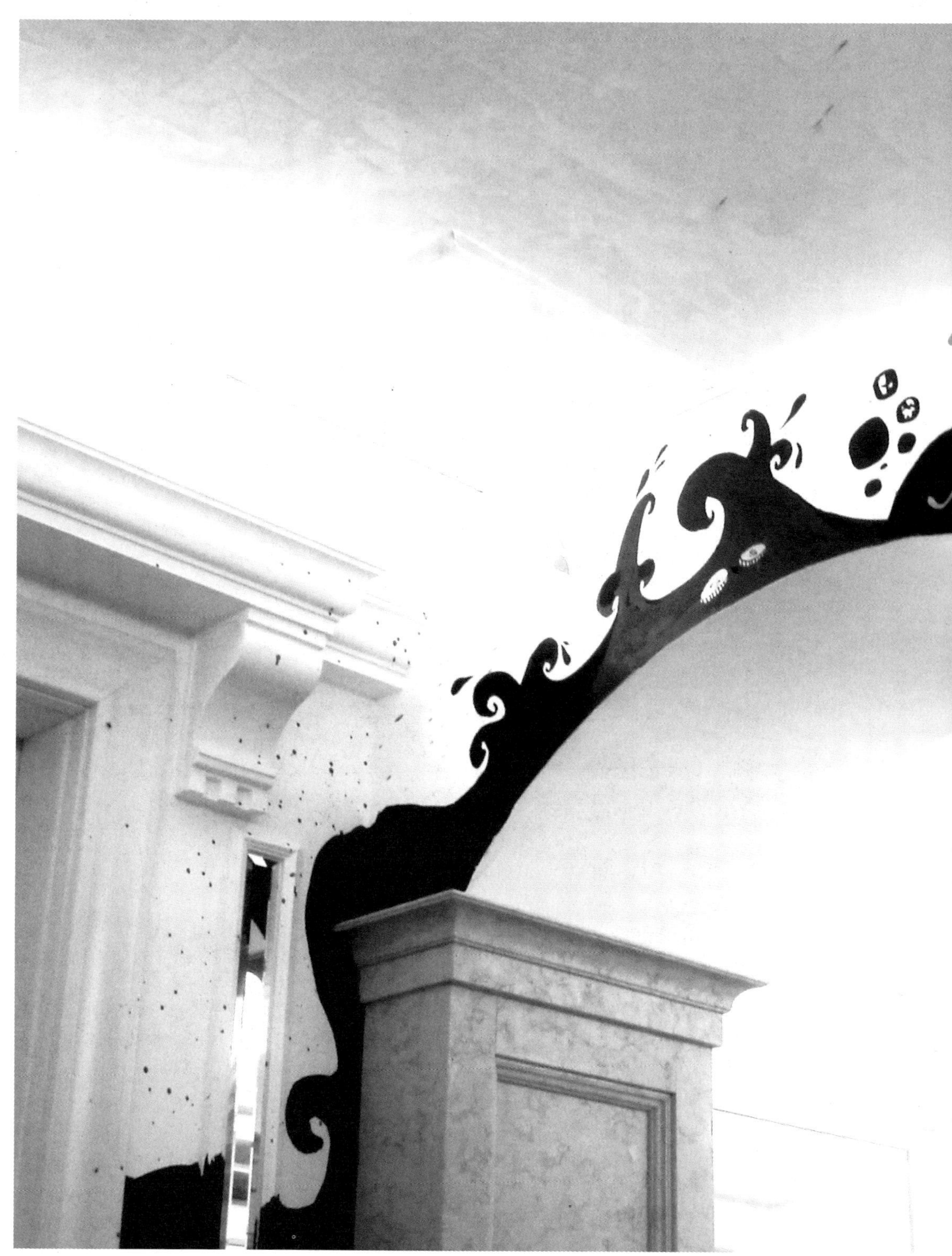

Byblos Art Hotel - Wallpaintings - Verona - 2007

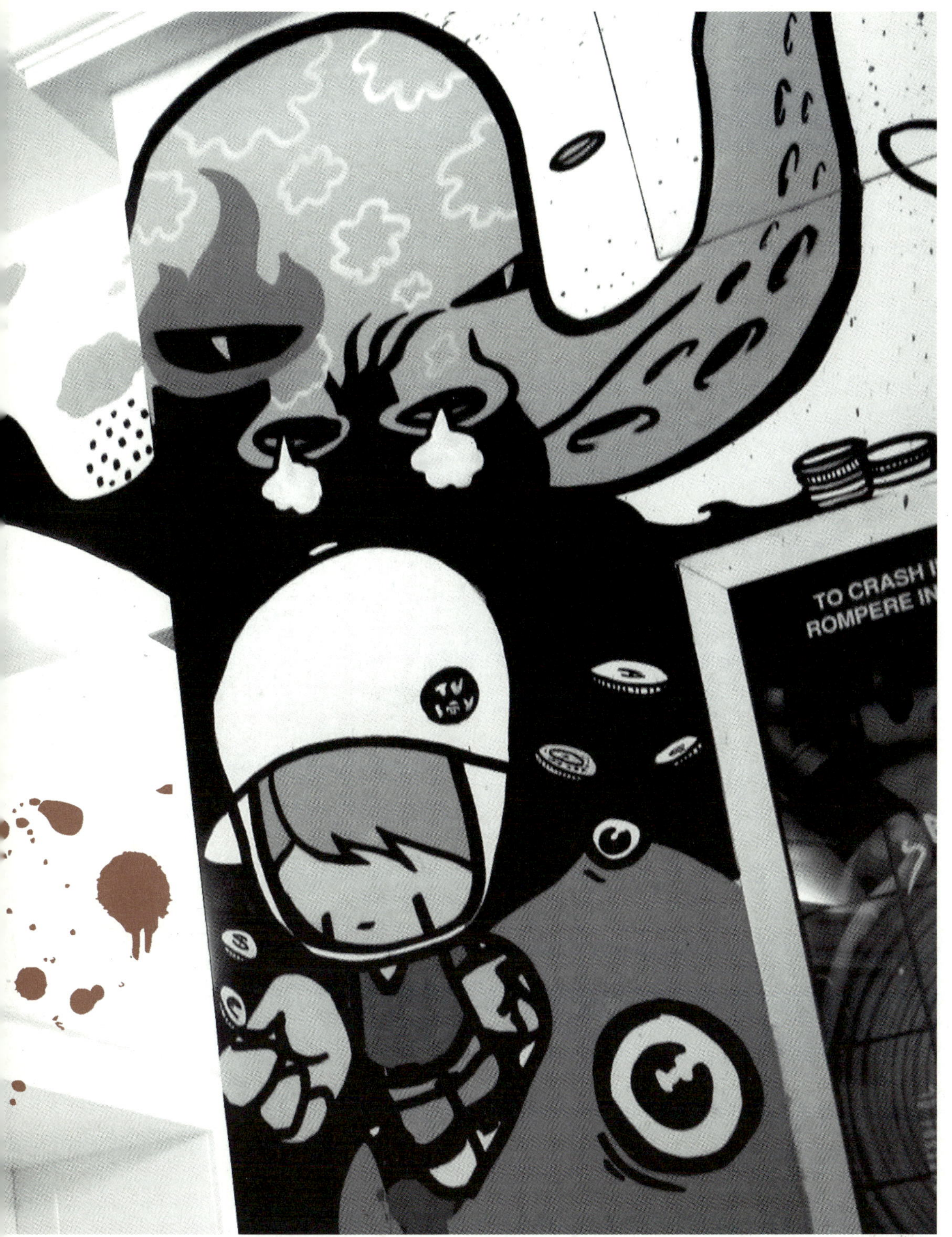
TO CRASH I
ROMPERE IN

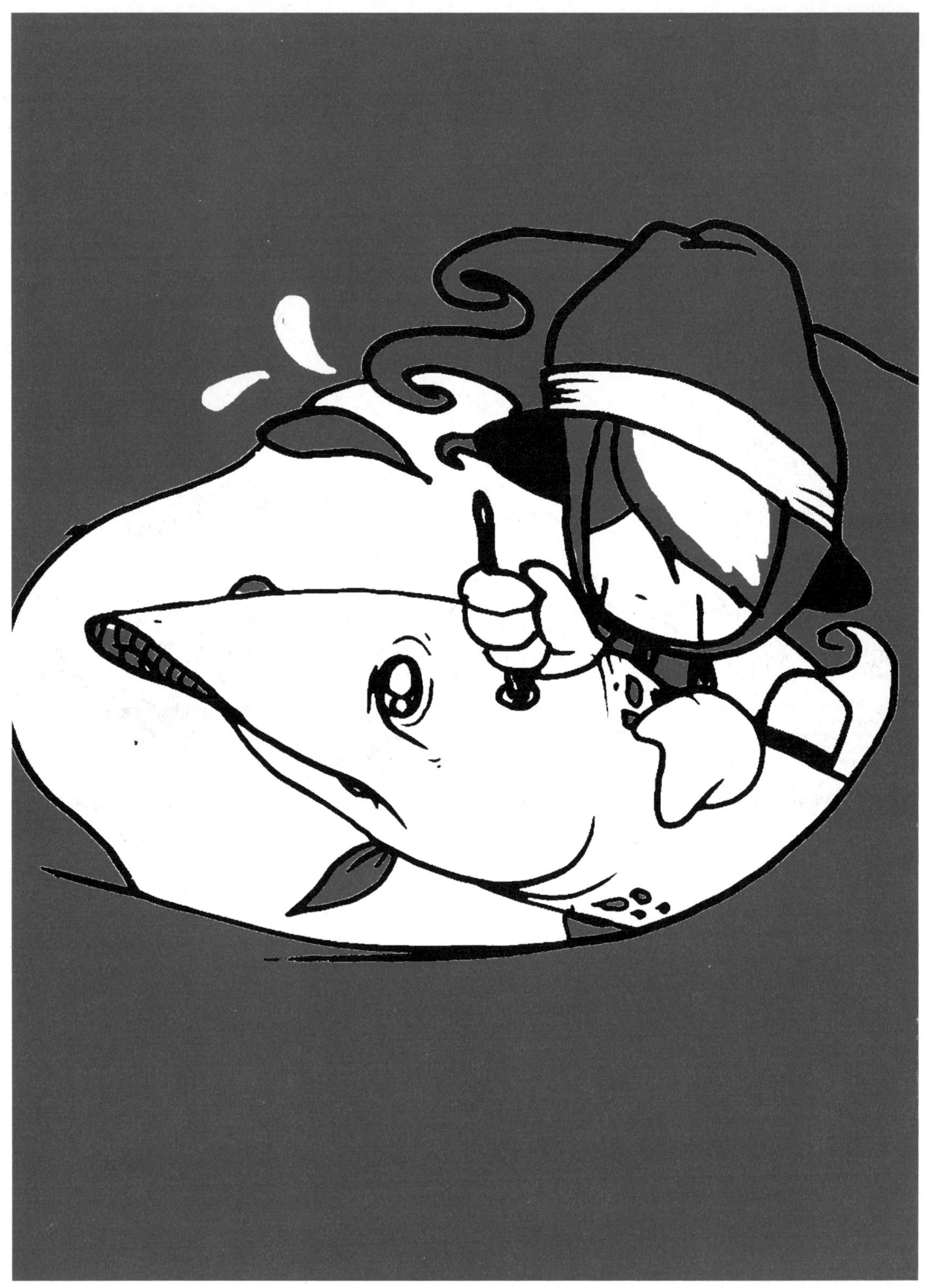

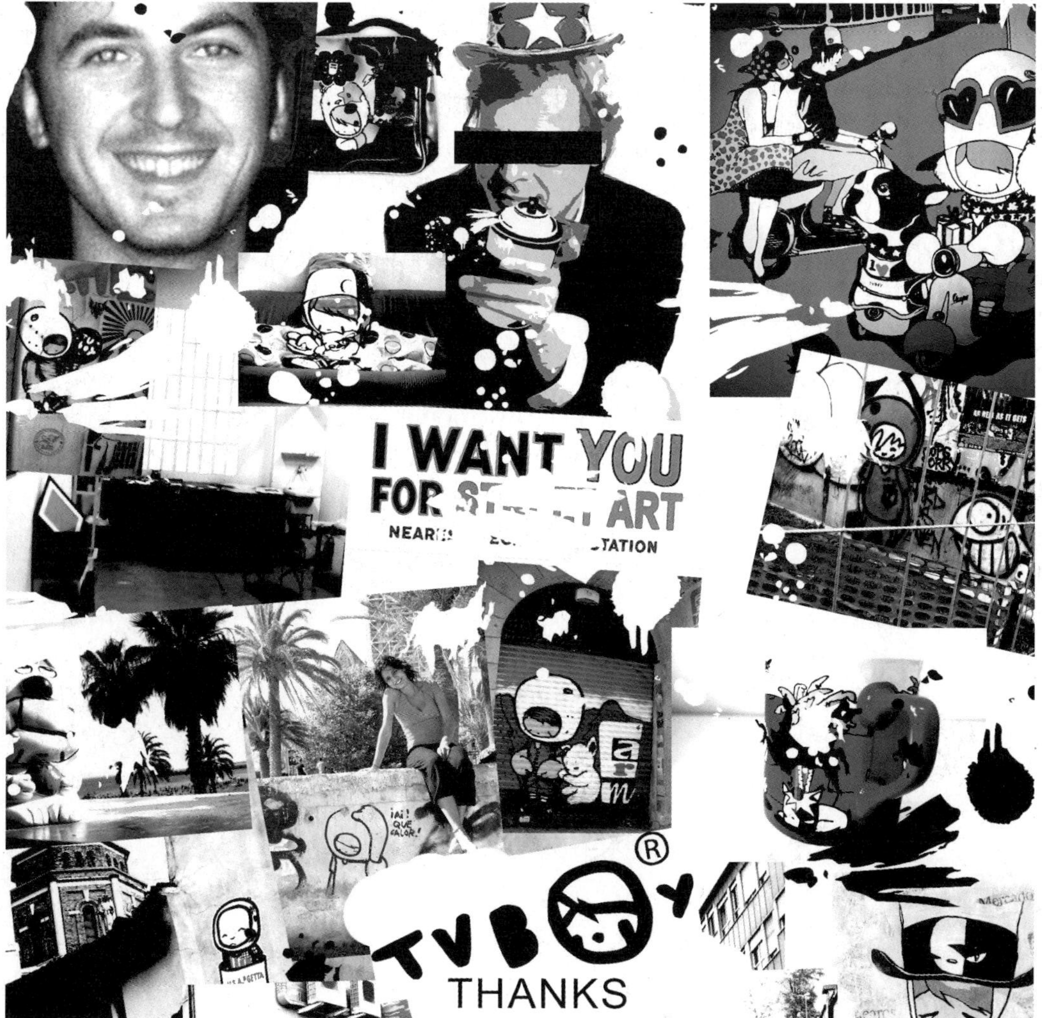

Thanks to:

My father for teaching me to draw and almost everything I know about art, my brother Sergio "Superfluo"
a great musician (!), my mother Anna, for her love, patience and support, Jacopo Perfetti from Art Kitchen
for his introduction text, Ivan for his poetry and enthusiasm, Nais, Pao and his out coming son, Maicol at
Pagano for his great help on our clothing project, Zak & Amedeo, my Italian mates in Bcn, Chaz, Iñigo,
Harlan, C100 and Eko for their text, Stefano & Masha at Byblos Art Gallery, Alessandro Riva for my first
one man exhibition, Giacomo Spazio, Oscar at Idep, Carlo Branzaglia, all the gallerists who helped me, all
thank you Drago for publishing my first book, my relatives in Sicily and my friends in Milan, all the street
artists I painted with and anyone I forgot, I beg your pardon...
To all the fans of TV Boy all the journalists who wrote or talked about my work, thanks so much for your
love and support!
To all the young and talented people who are making their first moves in the art world I would like to
say that this is a hard world to move in but it is surely better than being an employee in a boring and grey
company....don't give up!
To all liars, thieves and betrayers I met, beware of karma!

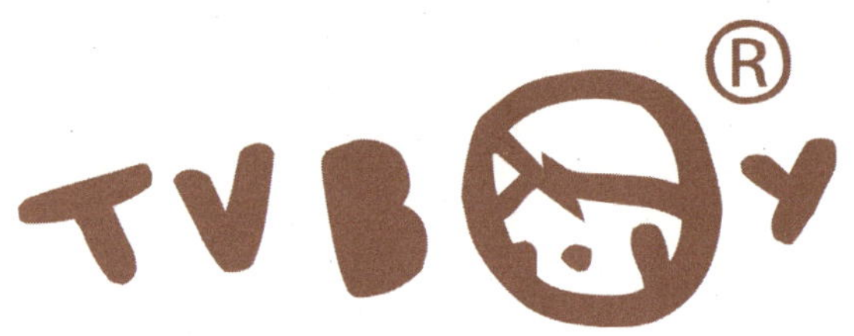

www.thetvboy.com

Published by: DRAGO
www.dragolab.it

All artwork copyright 2007 by TvBoy
All text ©Authors - All rights reserved
ISBN 978-88-88493-24-4
printed in italy

DRAGO Head Office, Rome Italy
E-mail: info@dragolab.it
Phone: +39 06 45439018 / +39 06 45439132
Fax: +39 06 45439159
Via Maria Adelaide 12, int. 9 - 00196, Rome, Italy
www.dragolab.it
For distribution inquieries: books@dragolab.it

North America
D.A.P./Distributed Art Publishers
155 Sixth Avenue, 2nd Floor
New York, N.Y. 10013
Tel: (212) 627-1999
Fax: (212) 627-9484
www.artbook.com
For sales: dwingate@dapinc.com
eleshowitz@dapinc.com
For press: agalan@dapinc.com

UK & Ireland, Scandinavia and non-exclusive Europe,
Far East, Middle East, Greece and Turkey
ART BOOKS INTERNATIONAL
Unit 200A, The Foundry
156 Blackfriars Road - London SE1 8EN
United Kingdom
Tel: 023 9220 0080
Fax: 023 9220 0090
For sales: keith@art-bks.com
For press: anne@art-bks.com

France and Belgium
CRITIQUES LIVRES DISTRIBUTION SAS
B. P. 93 24, rue Malmaison,
93172 Bagnolet cedex France
Tel: (01)43-60-39-10
Fax: (01)48-97-37-06
critiques.livres@wanadoo.fr

Italy
LIBRIMPORT SAS
Via Adda, 16/B
20090 Opera (Mi), Italy
Tel. +39 02 57605590
Fax: +39 02 57606002
librimport@libero.it

Spain, Portugal and Greece
BOOKPORT ASSOCIATES
via Luigi Salma, 7 - 20094 Corsico (MI), Italy
Tel : + 39 02 4510 3601
Fax : +39 024510 6426
bookport@bookport.it

Australia and New Zealand
BOOKWISE AUSTRALIA,
PUBLISHERS GROUP WORLDWIDE
174 Cormack Road - Wingfield, SA 5013
Cell: +61 419 340 056
www.bookwise.com.au
louise.griffin@bookwise.com.au

Germany, Austria, Switzerland and Netherlands
VISUAL BOOKS Sales Agency
Laubacher Str. 16 - D-14197 Berlin
Tel: +49 30 69819007
Fax: +49 30 69819005
service@visualbooks-sales.com